CALVIN VS WESLEY

BRINGING BELIEF IN LINE WITH PRACTICE

D O N   T H O R S E N

Abingdon Press
Nashville

CALVIN VS WESLEY
BRINGING BELIEF IN LINE WITH PRACTICE

Copyright © 2013 by Abingdon Press

Library of Congress Cataloging-in-Publication Data

Thorsen, Donald A. D.
    Calvin vs. Wesley : bringing belief in line with practice / Don Thorsen.
       pages   cm
    Includes bibliographical references and index.
    ISBN 978-1-4267-4335-1 (pbk. : alk. paper)   1. Wesleyan Church-Doctrines.   2. Methodist Church-Doctrines.   3. Wesley, John, 1703–1794.   4. Calvinism.   5. Reformed Church-Doctrines.   6. Calvin, Jean, 1509–1564.   I. Title.
    BX9995.W45T46 2013
    230'.7-dc23

                                                                              2013032318

15 16 17 18 19 20 21 22—10 9 8 7 6 5 4 3 2
MANUFACTURED IN THE UNITED STATES OF AMERICA

To my daughter

Heidi Thorsen.

May you continue to increase

"in wisdom and in years,

and in divine and human favor."

CONTENTS

PREFACE

For a long time, I have thought that Christians live remarkably similar to the way that John Wesley described Christianity and Christian living. However, Christians do not often understand or appreciate his insights into biblical teaching and the real-life ways that Christians live. It seems as if Wesley was very good at describing the Christian life in *practice,* but he was not as persuasive at describing it in *theory.* This discrepancy between theory and practice is unfortunate. It became apparent to me when I read a critique of Wesleyan spirituality by Glenn Hinson, who said, "Wesleyan thought has always come out better in practice than in theory."[1]

My background is Wesleyan. I grew up in a Free Methodist church, though I cannot say that everything I heard and observed was very Wesleyan. I attended Stanford University, which was certainly not Christian, much less Wesleyan. Then I attended Asbury Theological Seminary, where I first received extended theological and ministerial training in Wesley and Methodism. However, it was not until I did graduate studies in theology at Princeton Theological Seminary—a Reformed institution of higher education—that I became convinced of Wesleyan theology. Thereafter, I pursued doctoral studies in Wesley and Methodist studies at Drew University, where I earned my PhD in theological and religious studies.

Over the years, I have met many Christians outside the Wesleyan tradition. Very often they lived in a manner that was more like the way that Wesley described the Christian life than was reflective of their own theological tradition. In particular, I thought this to be true of Christians I met from the Reformed tradition that followed the theological leadership of John Calvin. Although they claimed to be Calvinist, they lived more like Wesley. In fact, I argue in this book that the majority of Protestant Christians with whom I am familiar, including those from Reformed traditions, live in practice more like the way that Wesley viewed God, the Bible, salvation, spirituality, the church, and ministry. If my thesis is correct, then Christians would do well to learn more about Wesley.

In this book, I endeavor to explain how well Wesley represents biblical

Christianity, holistically conceived, and to promote his beliefs, values, and practices. I consider them to be powerfully instructive for living lives that are both biblically based and practically relevant for people: individually and socially; spiritually and physically; ecclesiastically and ministerially. It is my hope that others will come to agree with me.

There are many people who I want to thank for helping me. I want to begin by thanking my editor, Kathy Armistead, for first challenging me with the prospect of writing this book. In addition, I am most grateful to Greg Crofford and my daughter Heidi Thorsen, who read my entire manuscript and gave invaluable counsel. I also want to thank friends and colleagues who gave me input on specific chapters. They include Larry Wood, Steve O'Malley, Don Dayton, Dennis Okholm, Heather Clements, Brian Lugioyo, Todd Pokrifka, Dan Clendenin, Bernie Van der Walle, Kurt Richardson, Sung Wook Chung, and Dave Bundy.

I also want to thank Ken Collins and Asbury Theological Seminary, who hosted the Wesleyan Studies Summer Seminar, where I began work on this book. Participants in the seminar gave helpful advice. They included Larry Wood, Steve O'Malley, Allan Coppedge, and Joe Dongell, who are faculty at the seminary. Seminar colleagues who contributed to my book included Greg Crofford, Phil Meadows, Bill Faupel, Tom Barlow, Soren Hessler, Ray Degenkolb, Tim Woolley, Rebecca Howell, Corey Markum, Susan Carole, and Chris Johnson.

I want to thank Azusa Pacific University, which provided a doctoral studies grant that helped pay for my travel to the Wesleyan Studies Summer Seminar. I also received university funding for research assistance, and I thank Chris Tansey for his help. In addition, I want to thank friends and colleagues at Azusa Pacific who provided encouragement for me in writing. They include Steve Wilkens, Keith Reeves, Brian Lugioyo, Scott Daniels, Kay Smith, Karen Winslow, Roger White, Keith Matthews, and Lynn Losie. Steve was especially helpful as a dialogue partner and coffee break enthusiast who contributed insight as well as humor throughout the writing process.

Finally, I want to thank my daughters, Liesl, Heidi, and Dana Thorsen, for their ongoing love, respect, and encouragement for my writing. They help motivate me to articulate in *theory* what I consider in *practice* to be invaluable for Christianity and Christian living. It is to my daughter Heidi that I dedicate this book.

ABBREVIATIONS

John Calvin

Commentaries *Calvin's Commentaries,* 22 vols., edited and translated by John King (1974 rpt.; Grand Rapids: Baker, 1993).

Institutes *Institutes of the Christian Religion* (1559), The Library of Christian Classics, vols. 20–21; edited by John T. McNeill; translated and indexed by Ford Lewis Battles (Philadelphia: Westminster, 1960); notations include both Calvin's system of numbering and the numbering in the two volumes (1–2).

Works *Selected Works of John Calvin: Tracts and Letters,* 7 vols., edited by Henry Beveridge and Jules Bonnet, translated by Henry Beveridge, et al. (Grand Rapids: Baker, 1983).

John Wesley

Letters (Telford) *The Letters of the Rev. John Wesley, A.M.,* 8 vols., edited by John Telford (London: Epworth, 1931).

NT Notes *Explanatory Notes Upon the New Testament,* 3rd corrected edition (Bristol: Graham and Pine, 1760–62; many later reprints).

Works *The Works of John Wesley;* begun as *The Oxford Edition of The Works of John Wesley* (Oxford: Clarendon, 1975-1983); continued as *The Bicentennial Edition of The Works of John Wesley* (Nashville: Abingdon, 1984); 18 of 35 vols. published to date.

Works (Jackson) *The Works of John Wesley,* 14 vols., edited by Thomas Jackson (London, 1872; Grand Rapids: Zondervan, 1958).

INTRODUCTION: CHRISTIANS LIVE MORE LIKE WESLEY THAN CALVIN

Although John Calvin profoundly influenced the development of Christianity, John Wesley did a better job than Calvin of conceptualizing and promoting Christian beliefs, values, and practices as described in the Bible and as lived by Protestant Christians. This claim may surprise people because Calvin is more often thought to speak theologically on behalf of Christianity, since he was a founding leader of the Protestant Reformation in the sixteenth century. Ironically, despite professed appeal that Christians may make to Calvin's theology, they often live in practice more like the teaching, preaching, and ministries of Wesley.

In this book, I want to emphasize how well Wesley understood and embodied biblical Christianity; I do not intend to put down Calvin. On the contrary, Wesley agreed with Calvin on many matters of Christianity. For example, Wesley famously said the following about his agreement with Calvin on the matter of justification by grace through faith: "I think on justification just as I have done any time these seven and twenty years, and just as Mr. Calvin does. In this respect I do not differ from him a hair's breadth."[1] Thus, if you—the reader—hope to find a methodical attack upon Calvin in this book, then you will be disappointed. Moreover, if you consider yourself a convinced Calvinist, then you may dislike this book. After all, preferring one person's theology over that of another is enough to upset some people personally as well as theologically. And this book decidedly falls on the side of Wesleyanism rather than that of Calvinism. Although I appreciate Calvin's contributions to Christianity, I argue that Wesley's theological understanding of the Bible and its application to Christian living are superior to those of Calvin.

Be that as it may, if you want to learn about differences between Wesley and Calvin, then you will learn much about the beliefs, values, and practices of the two church leaders, as well as why I consider Wesley more adept in understanding and applying biblical Christianity than Calvin. Moreover, if you want to understand why Wesley notably led one of the largest revivals in church history during the eighteenth century and why Wesleyan, Methodist, Holiness, Pentecostal, and other Christians continue to be profoundly influenced by him today, then you will certainly want to continue reading this book.

As Protestant Christians, Wesley and Calvin agreed with each other more than they disagreed. Both claimed to follow the heritage of biblical Christianity. Both claimed to follow the ancient creeds and teachings of key patristic writers; for example, they believed in divine creation, the doctrines of the Trinity and Incarnation, salvation, resurrection, eternal life, and so on. They had noteworthy disagreements with Roman Catholic interpretations of the creeds and patristic writers, but they tended to agree about why they disagreed with Catholics.[2] Finally, both claimed to be part of the resurgence of Christianity found in the Reformation and the Protestant traditions that followed them. Certainly both Wesley and Calvin were, and continue to be, foundational representatives of Protestantism. Thus, if for no other reason than to better understand the whole of Christianity, both Wesley and Calvin should be studied.

There exist differences, to be sure, between Wesley and Calvin. Otherwise, why would there be such divergent theological and church traditions descending from them? And, for the sake of distinguishing between the two men, it is important to note key points of contrast. Their differences represent crucial areas of disagreement that continued among Protestant Christians who followed them. Just as Wesley would consider some of the beliefs, values, and practices of Calvin to be wrong, so Calvin would think that Wesley was wrong. Wesley did not think that such differences precluded Calvin from being considered biblical and orthodox, but he did consider them crucial to spiritually fruitful Christian living. Perhaps if Calvin had had the opportunity to evaluate Wesley's beliefs, values, and practices, then he might have said the same about Wesley. We do not know, however, since Calvin lived two centuries prior to Wesley, and it is anachronistic—that is, historically out of place—to speculate.

During his lifetime, Wesley openly disagreed with followers of Calvin, though such disagreements did not preclude Wesley from ministering alongside them. Most notably, he disagreed with the Calvinist theology of George Whitefield. Whitefield was a lifelong friend of Wesley. Just as Wesley introduced Whitefield to the value of small group meetings and holy living, Whitefield introduced Wesley to the value of outdoor preaching and evangelism. Whitefield traveled to the American colonies where he helped spearhead the First Great Awakening. In Britain, Wesley led the Methodist revival, which similarly contributed to the spiritual renewal of the English-speaking world of the eighteenth century. Despite their public debate, both men affirmed and honored the ministries of each other to the amazement of those who observed them—Christians and non-Christians alike.

So talking about what Wesley got right and Calvin got wrong does not imply a knockdown, drag-out fight among Christians. But it does suggest an opportunity to see how the two leaders disagreed with each other, and why people follow the spiritual leadership of Wesley rather than that of Calvin. Indeed, one of the theses of this book is that a surprising number of those who claim to be Calvinist really live more like Wesley. Have Calvinists thought sufficiently through the implications of Calvin's theology relative to the way they actually live as Christians? Have other Christians thought sufficiently through the implications of their theology relative to the way they actually live as Christians? As the subtitle of this book suggests, studying Wesley will help Christians in "bringing belief in line with practice."

Theory and Practice

I think that one of the most difficult things in life for people to do is to live consistently, without hypocrisy. Many people, no doubt, would agree with that statement. But, ironically, they may agree with it for reasons different from what I intend. Most often they think that they possess correct beliefs and values, but they repeatedly fall short in living up to them in practice. For example, people may have a great conception of a healthy diet, but they lamentably fall short of following it; or people may understand how to budget their money, but for the life of them cannot live within that budget. The same thing holds true for them spiritually: people may imagine how they think they ought to live, based upon the Bible or other Christian values, but they repeatedly fall short of it. Usually such shortfallings are attributed to sin or the devil, and that may be the case. But it is not always our *practice*—our thoughts, words, and actions—that have fallen short; we may also be living lives deficient in theological *theory,* holding religious beliefs and values that weaken our Christian lives rather than strengthen us.

In addition, I argue that Christians may live better than they think—that is, better than they value what it is they think that they believe. For example, some people eat more healthily than they can describe theoretically or scientifically (not all people, mind you, but for some this is the case). Likewise, some people handle their budget and money or their time schedule and work responsibilities better than they could articulate in a formal, logical, or schedulelike manner. In fact, some people are relatively unaware of what they do, including what they do well. And, they would be better off if they had greater insight into what they actually believe and value. Because each of us has particular gifts, talents, and skills, some things just come more easily—perhaps consciously or unconsciously—than they do for others. In such cases, people would benefit from greater self-awareness or self-knowledge of what drives them spiritually, emotionally, intellectually, and relationally. To be sure, some people might be distraught if they discovered that their most cherished ideas do not fit their practice. But throughout this book I argue that the examined life far outweighs the unexamined life, and that people would do well to have their beliefs and values more similar than dissimilar with how they live in practice.

A repeated theme throughout this book is that Wesley provides a better understanding of Christianity and the Christian life in *practice* than Calvin does in *theory*. In other words, Wesley better captured the biblically described way that Christians live their lives—clarifying their spiritual challenges, hopes, and successes—than did Calvin. Because Wesley was not a systematically oriented theologian, as was Calvin, his theology has at times been belittled as being inferior to Calvin's theological logic and comprehensive system of belief. It is not that Wesley did not use logic, critical thinking, and persuasive argumentation; he just did not develop a system of theology per se. But Wesley did have a well-conceived and consistently lived theology.

Calvin's theological strength was also his greatest weakness. Life, including Christian life, is not necessarily something best described as a system—a logically constructed interconnection of beliefs and values. Such a description may be more applicable to rationalist philosophy or Christian scholasticism than to the Bible and to life. Whereas systematic theology is rationally appealing and culturally respectable, especially in Western society, Wesley's less systematic, more practically oriented approach to theology is more appropriate. This appropriateness is especially true when it comes to describing the dynamics of biblical Christianity in general, and in particular, of life in the Spirit—the Holy Spirit of God.

According to Wesley, one of the problems with a systematic approach to theology is that it may view Christianity too narrowly in terms of what fits into the system and what does not. For example, throughout his life, Wesley felt that Calvinists wrongly accused him of advocating works righteousness, when consistently Wesley advocated justification by grace through faith. Late in life, Wesley believed the problem was in part because of the narrow categories used in Calvinists' theological deliberations. He said:

> I was in this perplexity when a thought shot across my mind, which solved the matter at once: "This is the key: Those that hold, 'Every one is absolutely predestinated either to salvation or damnation', see no medium between salvation by works and salvation by absolute decrees." It follows, that whosoever denied salvation by absolute decrees, in so doing (according to their apprehension) asserts salvation by works.[3]

Wesley recognized that those who develop systems of Christian theology are heavily invested in logically rejecting beliefs and values that differ or perhaps challenge their system, even if affirming the system betrays biblical and commonsense evidence. It is not that Wesley was illogical and incoherent in developing his beliefs and values. After all, Wesley was a Fellow at Oxford University, taught logic, and used critical-thinking skills in crafting his writings. But his beliefs and values were not developed into a systematic whole that required apologetics and polemics in order to preserve a systemlike view of Christianity; Wesley's beliefs and values were more flexible, built upon a dynamic understanding of the ongoing presence of God's Holy Spirit in the lives of people.

Those who emphasize systematic theology are heavily invested in arguing propositionally that their beliefs and values are right and that other propositional beliefs and values are wrong, or they at least denounce them as slippery-slope arguments that eventually reveal their wrongness. Systematizers do not readily admit that Christian beliefs, values, and practices may vary from person to person and from church to church. They focus more on what can be rationally proved to be right or wrong, consistent or inconsistent, regardless of commensurability with real-life circumstances, questions, and concerns. However, from Wesley's perspective, system-making and proposition-based apologetics and polemics too often fail to capture the Spirit-led vitality of what he called "religion of the heart"—a concept too categorically unsystematic and Spirit-oriented for Calvinists.[4]

Calvin, of course, spoke of the Holy Spirit and of mysteries involved with Christianity. It is not as if he did not account for such paradoxes of faith. Calvin was intellectually aware and astute with regard to historic theological disputation. But for Calvin, the rational unity of his theology superseded the vagaries of individual experiences of faith, hope, love, and other Spirit-led encounters with God and others. To be sure, mysteries and paradoxes existed in Calvin's theology, but they were considered inconsequential relative to the excellences of the explanatory power of his systematic theology.

In the ancient church, the phrase *complexio oppositorum* (Latin, "the complex of opposites") was used to describe theological affirmations that seemingly hold together contradictory propositions. For example, because God is ultimately thought to transcend all human descriptions (even biblical descriptions), there exists necessarily a degree of mystery or paradox regarding Christian descriptions of God, who immanently interacts with people. The same complexity could be said to be true of the theology of Calvin (or of any Christian theologian, for that matter). After all, Calvin systematically portrayed God and all matters related to God in a way that honored the transcendence of God while at the same time doing justice to the immanent presence and relationality of God. Because Christians "walk by faith, not by sight" (2 Corinthians 5:7), attempts to explain God fully—including those of Calvin—have been eschewed. Despite this complexity, Christians have also been confident of the degree to which God and God's decrees may truthfully be understood and communicated to others. Calvin represents one of the more confident theologians in terms of the certainty with which doctrinal pronouncements can be made about God and the works of God. That does not mean that sophistication and nuance are not important in studying Calvin; they are. But more than most, Calvin thought that God and all matters related to God can be pronounced with confidence, even if it means that there are some questions and concerns that Christians ought to avoid, since these questions and concerns do not fit into a systematic whole.

Despite Wesley's more practical approach to theology, he better understood, responded to, and gave leadership to the challenges that people face. These challenges include the way the Holy Spirit leads, guides, and empowers people, and how people need to be faithful in the way they live in response to God, the Bible, and loving their neighbor as themselves. Calvin's partiality for system-making is not the highest Christian value, and making it so loses more of the dynamic of Christian life than reason and logic contribute. Again, this does not mean that rationality, reason, and logic are unimportant; it just means that they ought not to be given higher value than faith, hope, and love, which are more relational than rational in nature. And relationships, after all, can be rather messy or inexact when it comes to describing them, including our relationship with God. This does not mean that Christians ought not to try adeptly to understand God, themselves, their relationships, and other religious matters. But there needs to be greater willingness to investigate the messiness of Christianity, including all its mysteries and paradoxes, than not to do so.

Wesley wisely knew the need to hold in tension opposites often held apart. William Abraham describes Wesley and his theology in the following way:

Wesley's significance as a theologian rests fundamentally on his ability to hold together elements in the Christian tradition that generally are pulled apart and expressed in isolation. Thus he integrates contrasting emphases that are vital to a healthy and comprehensive vision of the Christian faith.

Consider the following disjunctive pairs: faith, works; personal devotions, sacramental practice; personal piety, social concern; justification, sanctification; evangelism, Christian nurture; Bible, tradition; revelation, reason; commitment, civility; creation, redemption; cell group, institutional church; local scene, world parish.[5]

As a result of Wesley's practical and integrative approach to understanding biblical Christianity, his theology was existentially relevant and applicable, even if not always stated with the precise categorization of a systematic theology.

In Praise of Calvin

John Calvin (1509–64) was undeniably one of the most influential Christian leaders of all time, not just of the Protestant Reformation. Along with Martin Luther and Ulrich Zwingli, Calvin was one of the towering figures of the spiritual resurgence of Christianity in Continental Europe during the sixteenth century. He was a prodigious writer who most notably lived and worked in Geneva, where he gave leadership to the Swiss churches that initiated the Reformed tradition of Protestantism. Following the theological and ecclesiastical leadership of Zwingli and William Farel, Calvin regularly preached and taught in the Genevan churches. He was an apologist for Protestantism, and his writings served to establish the Reformed movement, which separated from the ecclesiastical and political authority of the Roman Catholic Church. Calvin was also polemical, at times, when he considered it necessary to challenge alternative Christian ideas and actions that he considered heretical or a threat to the Reformed understanding of biblical Christianity.

One of his greatest legacies was the writing of the *Institutes of the Christian Religion*, which he first published with six chapters in 1536. Throughout his lifetime, Calvin revised the *Institutes* several times, occasionally expanding its length and other times adding chapters. He published his final edition in 1559; it contained eighty chapters that were divided into four volumes or books. Generally speaking, the first book dealt with God and creation; the second book dealt with Jesus Christ and redemption; the third book dealt with the Holy Spirit and justification by faith; and the fourth book dealt with the church and ministry. It is difficult to calculate how significant the *Institutes* has been in shaping countless lives and congregations for half a millennium. In a single publication, Calvin was able to distill his basic theological beliefs, moral values, and ministerial practices. If anyone wanted a publication to which he or she could turn in order to understand the essence of Reformed theology, then the *Institutes* provided a single source for understanding it. If an individual Christian or church could turn to only one corpus, other than the Bible, for articulating his, her, or its faith, then Calvin's *Institutes* represented a comprehensive, systematic compendium of beliefs, values, and practices that could be used with authority among Protestant Christians.

Along with the *Institutes,* Calvin encouraged people to study the Bible commentaries he wrote. Calvin published exegetical commentaries on almost all of the New Testament and much of the Old Testament. The commentaries helped people study the Bible more in depth as they endeavored to understand Christianity in a post–Roman Catholic, post–Holy Roman Empire context. In addition, Calvin published sermons, created catechisms, and even wrote hymns for the worship and nurture of those in churches. To further serve people, Calvin instituted a place of Christian education, which included a *collège* for the instruction of children and an *académie* for the advanced education of students. He sent out pastors as missionaries, especially to his home country of France, and oversaw the *consistoire* (or council), which served as an ecclesiastical court for deciding upon matters of Christian belief, values, and practices, even exercising the authority to censure, excommunicate, and more with regard to those deemed heretical. To these accomplishments, others could easily be added, including the influence Calvin had upon the expanding Protestant movement throughout Continental Europe and Britain. Understandably, Calvin never saw the full extent of his influence, since it continues to grow to this day.

In Praise of Wesley

John Wesley (1703–91) lived approximately two centuries after Calvin. In many ways, their social, political, and church contexts were dramatically different, and these differences must be kept in mind when comparing the two leaders. During his lifetime, Calvin was more involved with establishing the church of Geneva against centuries of Roman Catholic power, which was political as well as ecclesiastical. Wesley, however, was more involved with renewing the Church of England—the Anglican Church—which he argued had lost its spiritual vitality. Calvin wanted to defend zealously and argue clearly for the Reformed tradition, whereas Wesley wanted to evangelize and fashion effective means of spiritual formation. Of course, Wesley and Calvin were also similar in ways. Both were resolutely biblical; both were dedicated to the well-being of the church; and both endeavored to spread their beliefs, values, and practices.

Wesley was an ordained Anglican minister who served as a missionary, was an Oxford Fellow, and eventually—with his brother Charles—became one of the cofounders of Methodism. Methodism was a Christian renewal movement that revived people in Britain as well as the newly established United States of America. Methodism functioned like an order within the Anglican Church, with Methodist societies that met midweek, and with class meetings and select bands that provided small accountability groups for the promotion of holy living and ministry. He appointed itinerant ministers who traveled widely to support Methodist societies, including men and women who served as local lay ministers. Wesley promoted evangelism, missions, and various social ministries. In addition to creating schools and orphanages for children, he advocated on behalf of prison reform and the abolition of slavery.

Although Wesley may be best known for his leadership in Methodism, he was also a prolific writer. As a minister, he wrote many sermons, compiling more than 150 into his collections of sermons along with *Explanatory Notes upon the New Testament,* which served as doctrinal guides for the Methodists. In addition, Wesley published his letters, a series of journals that spanned almost fifty years of his life, and a thirty-volume anthology of Christian writings entitled *A Christian Library* containing "Extracts from and Abridgments of the Choicest Pieces of Practical Divinity Which Have Been Published in the English Tongue." Wesley did not write a systematic theology; instead, he claimed to speak "*ad populum*—to the bulk of mankind—to those who neither relish nor understand the art of thinking, but who notwithstanding are competent judges of those truths which are necessary to present and future happiness."[6] Consequently, Wesley published multiple volumes of Christian literature that Christians and churches continue to use.

Comparing Wesley and Calvin

In comparing Wesley and Calvin, I do not intend to discuss all of their beliefs, values, and practices. Instead, I plan to focus on some of the fundamental differences between them, and the implications of those differences in how they understood the church and ministry. This approach will still highlight key theological affirmations of both Wesley and Calvin. Readers may be assured that they will study the essence of both men's understanding of God, humanity, sin, salvation, the church, and ministry. Not every doctrine will be studied, but a great breadth of their beliefs, values, and practices will be discussed.

I will focus primarily on the writings of Wesley and Calvin, rather than upon secondary literature about them. This will be easy since both men were prolific authors. I will bring in secondary literature about the two men when it is appropriate, especially when it has to do with their respective historical contexts, but I mostly will focus on the primary writings of Wesley and Calvin.

I plan to avoid later developments of "Calvinism" and "Wesleyanism," as they developed after the time of the respective leaders. To be sure, we sometimes hear more about Calvinism and the Reformed traditions than about Calvin, and more about Wesleyanism and the Methodist traditions than about Wesley. These offshoots can reveal a great deal about their founders, sometimes revealing insights or implications about which the founders were unconcerned or, perhaps, unaware. Other times the followers of Calvin and Wesley—Calvinists and Wesleyans—misrepresent and even distort the ideas of the founders. Although such information can be of help in understanding Calvin and Wesley, it will not be the focus of this book. Instead I will focus on the original writings of the two leaders.

More Than, Less Than

In evaluating Wesley and Calvin, my approach will be to talk about them with regard to how they view different beliefs and values of Christianity, especially those that directly influence the lives of Christians. Thus, I will begin by discussing how they viewed God and the Bible, since these are basic to the Christian life. I will proceed by talking about how Wesley and Calvin viewed humanity, grace, salvation, and spirituality. Finally, I will talk about how they viewed the church and other issues related to ministry.

I will spend more time talking about the writings of Wesley and Calvin than about their interpretive treatments of the Bible per se. This may disappoint some readers, since they want to look more closely at how each man dealt with particular biblical passages. Some of those passages will, of course, be investigated. However, both Wesley and Calvin claimed that their beliefs, values, and practices were based primarily on the Bible. It is not a matter of whether one was more biblical than another; both were thoroughly knowledgeable of the Bible and built their respective theologies upon it. They simply did not agree with each other's interpretation, and so the focus of this book will be more upon comparing and contrasting their biblical understandings than upon doing biblical exegesis.

Comparisons will reveal that Wesley and Calvin have more in common than not. However, it is the differences that will be focused upon more often, not because I want to be contentious but because it is the way that must be followed in order to contrast the two and to highlight their distinctiveness—what makes them stand out among others in church history. Without doubt, some of the differences became major points of contention among later Protestants. Some of the theological debates arose during the life of Calvin; by the time of Wesley, theological debates definitely occurred. Even during the life of Calvin, such debates ended in far more than hurt feelings; excommunication, banishments, and even executions occurred. Today, debates over the same kinds of issues about which Wesley and Calvin disagreed continue to divide Christians. So the comparison of Wesley and Calvin is not a moot historical reminiscence without contemporary relevance. On the contrary, Christians ought to be aware of the theological issues involved so that they may become more informed as well as adept in deciding for themselves about the topics of debate. Although we may find it difficult to decide, the issues are too important to ignore. In fact, who we find to be more persuasive—Wesley or Calvin—may have far-reaching implications for how we live as Christians and minister to others.

In comparing Wesley and Calvin, my approach will be to show emphases between the beliefs, values, and practices of the two Christian leaders. I will try to avoid setting up either-or comparisons, though in some instances it is unavoidable. Such dualistic thinking—or "either-or-ism," as I call it—can damage accurate descriptions of the views of both Wesley and Calvin. Although I side with Wesley, rather than Calvin, I try to be fair to the views of both men so that comparisons are genuine, rather than contrived. It is not fair to set up a "straw person," so to speak, which does not accurately describe the views of Calvin, just to knock it down. On the contrary, I think that there are enough genuine differences between Wesley and Calvin so that contrasts do not need to be manufactured. If readers think that I err in presenting Calvin—or Wesley, for that matter—then I apologize and am willing to be corrected. At least, it has been my intent to be as accurate and fair as possible.

For example, in talking about how Wesley and Calvin viewed God, both of them believed in the sovereignty of God. Both believed that God is all-powerful, and both believed that God is loving. It is not that they do not believe in these things about God; it is more about how they believe them. Wesley, I argue, puts more emphasis on the love of God than upon the power of God, and Calvin puts more emphasis on the power of God than upon the love of God. This does not mean that Wesley never talks about the power of God and that Calvin never talks about the love of God. So, one may find individual references in Wesley and Calvin that seem to contradict what I say about them. However, individual references from either Wesley or Calvin do not necessarily refute my theses. (Likewise, individual references from the Bible used to support either Wesley or Calvin do not necessarily refute my theses, since both leaders appealed to the same Bible and verses; Wesley and Calvin just interpreted them differently.) Again, the contrasts between Wesley and Calvin are sometimes more a matter of emphasis (prominence, accent, or flavor) than of binary, either-or thinking with regard to comparing them.

Emphases, of course, are difficult to establish. In doing so, I will present quotations from both Wesley and Calvin in order to make my points. Such references are not intended to be slam-dunk proof of my theses, utilizing eisegesis (proof-texting) rather than exegesis of the writings of the two leaders. Instead, they are intended to represent accurately the theologies of Wesley and Calvin. This book is not intended to be an exhaustive theological survey, but it does intend to be reasonable in representing essential beliefs, values, and practices of both leaders, which would be born out through more extensive study of Wesley and Calvin.

Each chapter begins by talking about Calvin's views of a subject. I continue by talking about Wesley's views, and then I compare and contrast the two. In each chapter I draw out implications of the beliefs and values of each man, since their implications are as important as their rational, propositional, or confessional value. Right belief (or what some refer to as *orthodoxy*: Latin, *ortho,* "right" + *doxy,* "glory, teaching, belief") has long been considered foundational to Christianity, but so have other dimensions of it. Other Christian values include right action (*orthopraxy*), a right heart (*orthokardia*), and a right society (*orthosocietas*).[7] Christianity ought not to be understood one-dimensionally; it is holistic, embracing the whole of God's creation and redemptive work in the world. Throughout the book, I will discuss these ideas as ways for developing a broader, more relevant, and effective way of understanding God, Christianity, and the ways God intends for us to live, based upon biblical teaching as well as historic Christianity and personal experience.

Appendix: TULIP and ACURA

In the appendix, I will talk about the so-called five points of Calvinism, which arose in the century after Calvin passed away. In the Netherlands, debate festered among the followers of Calvin and the followers of James Arminius, all of whom were part of the Reformed tradition of Protestantism. At the Synod of Dort, Arminius's followers—the Remonstrants—expected to debate their differences with the governing Calvinists but ended up being condemned for their beliefs. Points of disagreement became known as the "five points of Calvinism," which in English have been summarized with the acrostic TULIP. The acrostic stands for (1) total depravity, (2) unconditional election, (3) limited atonement, (4) irresistible grace, and (5) perseverance of the saints. It is debatable, of course, whether the five points of Calvinism accurately represents the views of Calvin. The Synod of Dort debate will not be addressed in this book until the appendix, but the substance of the issues will appear as Calvin discussed them in his writings.

Although Calvinists today often refer to the five points of Calvinism as a shorthand way to distinguish their beliefs, values, and practices from those of others, I do not think that all self-described Calvinists live in accordance with them. That is why some followers of Calvin call themselves four-point, three-point, two-point, and—in some instances—one-and-a-half-point Calvinists or less! When these followers of Calvin follow so few points reflective of his systematic theology, one wonders why they continue to call themselves Calvinist. After all, so many of Calvin's views as well as those individuals who follow him rely upon the logical interconnectedness between the theological components of his system of beliefs.

Wesley, however, did not disagree altogether with every part of the five points of Calvinism. So it is inappropriate to compare Wesley and Calvin based upon this fivefold criterion. Nor is it accurate theologically to interpret Wesley as an Arminian, since the Calvinist-Arminian categories represent the debate that originated within the Reformed tradition of Continental Europe.

Wesley's theological background did not come primarily from Continental Europe and the magisterial Protestant Reformation of Luther and Calvin. It came more from the Anglican tradition, which drew deeply from the *catholic* (or universal) traditions of Christianity, including Roman Catholic, Orthodox, and Protestant churches. As such, I refer to Wesley's theological tradition as *Anglo-Catholicism,* since it was formed by more ancient church traditions than the Continental Reformation. After all, the word *catholic* served in history to describe the universal, worldwide church and not any particular branch of it. For example, the word *catholic* prominently appeared in the first formal Christian creed—the Nicene Creed in the fourth century—along with the words *one, holy,* and *apostolic* in description (or marks) of the church.

Not everyone is familiar with the term *Anglo-Catholicism,* and it may be confusing to Protestants who think—by definition—that they are supposed to oppose anything that smacks of "Catholic" or "Catholicism." This kind of knee-jerk reaction, however, is unfortunate because it overlooks so much of the historical influence that the Church of England had upon Wesley as well as upon many other Christians in the English-speaking world. Thus, in order to understand Wesley, one should not impose upon him theological terms and doctrines representative of Reformed or even Arminian Christianity. Such an imposition will misunderstand and misrepresent his beliefs, values, and practices. Wesley's theological views arose within the broader context of Anglo-Catholic theological influences in Britain and not only that of Continental Europe. In his later life, Wesley identified with Arminianism as being similar to his theological concerns, especially in dispute with Calvinists. But the theology that shaped his ministries came more through the Anglo and catholic Christian traditions that preceded or paralleled the Continental Reformation.

This misunderstanding of Wesley's theological context especially confuses followers of Luther and Calvin, since the words, doctrines, and ministries of Wesley do not easily fit into the theological categories of the Continental Reformation. And, what people do not understand, they may all-too-quickly judge as being wrong or worse! But not all of Protestantism fits into Lutheran and Reformed (especially Calvinist) categories. Christians would be wise to consider a more historically and theologically complex understanding of Protestantism that does not always stem directly from Continental Europe. Thus, Anglo-Catholic categories must be given primary consideration in order to appreciate adequately the beliefs, values, and practices of Wesley.

If people insist on using the five points of Calvinism as the means by which to compare Wesley and Calvin, as historically and theologically inappropriate as it is, then the appendix in this book may be of help to them. As already mentioned, one of the reasons Calvinism is so appealing is because of its rational, systematic appeal. It is so logical that its basic beliefs can point by point be presented, and organized thinking on any topic impresses people. In my opinion, one of the reasons why people do not regard Arminian-oriented theologies (reflective of more ancient Catholic, Orthodox, and Anglican theologies) more highly is because there is not a nice, neat acrostic with which to remember the views contrary to the five points of Calvinism. That is why I created an alternative acrostic: ACURA. It stands for (1) all are sinful, (2) conditional election, (3) unlimited atonement, (4) resistible grace, and (5) assurance of salvation.[8] The acrostic may sound clichéd. But it helps people remember differences between Calvin (and his followers) and those who disagreed. Among those who disagreed were Arminius, Wesley, and a host of other people, including many who lived long before Calvin. It is my hope that, as people read the appendix, they will find, when they take the time to think about the theological issues involved, that the substance of ACURA far better applies to how they believe and live than does TULIP.

Discussion Questions

1. Although this may be the first time you have read about John Calvin, what do you know about him and about his Calvinist followers?

2. What do you know about John Wesley and his Wesleyan followers, which include people from the Methodist, Holiness, and other traditions?

3. To what degree do your beliefs and values (theory) correlate with how you live (practice)? Why do you think that this is the case? How might your theory and practice become more complementary?

4. When you think of Christianity, how do you envision it? Is it more like a system? A way of life? Or some combination of them?

5. What is most important: Right beliefs? Right practice? Right heart? Right society? All equally, or is there an order in their value?

6. Although I will not discuss the comparison between Calvinism and Arminianism until the end of the book, have you heard about the five points of Calvinism and Arminianism? What are your thoughts about them?

Chapter 1

GOD: MORE LOVE THAN SOVEREIGNTY

*Beloved, let us love one another, because love is from God; everyone who loves is
born of God and knows God. Whoever does not love does not know God,
for God is love. (1 John 4:7-8)*

When I was in seminary, a roommate of mine signed up for CPE—
Clinical Pastoral Education. His particular supervised ministry
was to serve as a chaplain in a state university hospital. On the first day, his
supervisor sent the student chaplains out onto their hospital floors without
much instruction. Upon return, the student chaplains lamented that they
were unsure about how to minister to patients. Should they pray for the
patients? If they prayed, then how should they pray? For physical healing?
For spiritual healing? For encouragement to persevere? For quality care from
their physicians? Or, should they not pray but minister to patients more with
the gifts of presence, conversation, or advocacy on behalf of their particular
needs?

The supervisor responded to the student chaplains by asking the question, What is your view of God? If you believe that all things happen according to the will of God, then you will pray that God's will be done. If you
believe in a God who heals, then you will pray for healing. If you believe in
a God who helps people help themselves, then you will pray for spiritual,
physical, and emotional strength for the patients. If you do not believe in a
God who answers prayers, then you will concentrate more on being present
with patients, conversing with them, and advocating for them.

This story profoundly influenced me as a seminarian because it made
me realize how important my view of God is. How do you view God? As

Christians, how we view God affects all aspects of our lives. For example, it affects how much or how little we think that God is actively involved in our salvation. Just as important, it affects how much or how little we think that God is actively involved in our day-to-day lives. Is God very much or a little involved? How is God involved? What priorities does God have, and what ends is God trying to achieve? Is God's will primarily for our individual benefit, or for the benefit of the church? Or, are there grander plans involved, which may or may not directly affect us as individuals? Do God's plans include society, all countries, and the environment?

These questions and others like them profoundly affect our lives as well as our understanding of Christianity. They influence what we think about God, just as our basic beliefs about God influence us daily—who we are as well as what we think, say, and do. We ought not to minimize our views of God, even if we are not always knowingly aware of them. Beliefs about God, whether we are consciously or unconsciously aware of them, powerfully affect us. They influence who we are and how we relate with others in the world and with ourselves and not just how we relate with God. Thus, in comparing Wesley and Calvin, it is important to begin with how they each viewed God.

Calvin's View of God

Calvin believed in the absolute sovereignty of God. From his perspective, Christians ought to do all they can to acknowledge God's almighty power, to celebrate the glory of God, and to give praise and thanks for how God directs all that occurs. In the opening passage of the *Institutes,* Calvin says:

> *Nearly all the wisdom we possess, that is to say, true and sound wisdom, consists of two parts: the knowledge of God and of ourselves. But, while joined by many bonds, which one precedes and brings forth the other is not easy to discern. In the first place, no one can look upon himself without immediately turning his thoughts to the contemplation of God, in whom he "lives and moves" [Acts 17:28]. For, quite clearly, the mighty gifts with which we are endowed are hardly from ourselves; indeed, our very being is nothing but subsistence in the one God.*[1]

Calvin did all he could to honor God's majesty, and it influenced every dimension of his beliefs, values, and practices.

This sovereign view of God makes complete sense to Christians. How often have you heard people say that they "give all the glory to God?" They do not want to take credit for any good thing that happens; instead, they give praise and thanks to God for who God is and for all that God has done for them: creating them, providentially caring for them, and redeeming them.

2

Why would people ever want to take anything away from the sovereignty, majesty, glory, and power of God?

From Calvin's perspective, these affirmations about God are firmly taught in the Bible, or as he usually referred to it, Scripture. Verse after verse can be found that talks about the supremacy of God: God's power; God's knowledge; God's presence. Calvin especially spoke of God's power, which he referred to as "God's omnipotence." Calvin said:

> For he is deemed omnipotent, not because he can indeed act, yet sometimes ceases and sits in idleness, or continues by a general impulse that order of nature which he previously appointed; but because, governing heaven and earth by his providence, he so regulates all things that nothing takes place without his deliberation. For when, in The Psalms, it is said that "he does whatever he wills" [Ps. 115:3; cf. Ps. 113: 3, Vg.], a certain and deliberate will is meant.[2]

Calvin's doctrine of providence reflects his high regard for the sovereignty of God. Providence has to do with God's ongoing care for creation. So great is God's care for the world and for people God created that nothing takes place without divine oversight. Calvin said: "At the outset, then, let my readers grasp that providence means not that by which God idly observes from heaven what takes place on earth, but that by which, as keeper of the keys, he governs all events."[3] He continued: "To sum up, since God's will is said to be the cause of all things, I have made his providence the determinative principle for all human plans and works, not only in order to display its force in the elect, who are ruled by the Holy Spirit, but also to compel the reprobate to obedience."[4] Thus, Calvin thought that the sovereignty of God is a blessing, a comfort, and encouragement to people, especially to Christians, because they are not alone. They are not without an omnipotent God who oversees and purposefully works in their lives. Indeed, God's sovereignty and providence represent Calvin's "determinative principle."

In talking about the providence of God, Calvin raised the issue of the reprobate—that is, one who will suffer eternal damnation. If God controls all that occurs, then why is it that some are reprobate? Clearly Calvin believes that the future of all, including the reprobate, occurs by the will or decrees of God, which occurred before the world was created. He said, "God once established by his eternal and unchangeable plan those whom he long before determined once for all to receive into salvation, and those whom, on the other hand, he would devote to destruction."[5] Calvin continued, "Therefore, those whom God passes over, he condemns; and this he does for no other reason than that he wills to exclude them from the inheritance which he predestines for his own children."[6] He was aware of the logical implications of these affirmations, and actually admitted, "The decree is dreadful indeed, I confess."[7] However, he considered the affirmation of God's sovereignty and the omnipotent purposes of God to transcend those of finite human minds and that people ought to approach all the works of God with humble submission, intellectually as well as volitionally.

Rather than being a liability to faith, Calvin considered the omnipotent providence of God to be an enormous benefit, an encouragement to those who believe, because ultimately God is in control of all that occurs. Because of human finitude and sin, it is a relief to know that God saves people, rather than people having to rely upon any human potentiality for securing salvation. Praise and thanks be to God, who redeems us when we do not have the wherewithal to redeem ourselves!

Calvin saw no contradiction between saying that God determines all that happens and saying that sinners—that means everyone—are accountable for sin. It is finally they who succumb to temptation, and not God; people commit the sinful acts. No doubt mystery surrounds this affirmation, but the clear teachings of the Bible deny that God is the cause of sin. Certainly, Christian faith demands that people affirm the teachings of the Bible, rather than try in their human, finite, sin-tainted ways to resolve questions of ultimate responsibility for sin. Rather than God, it is Satan and demons who are the immediate instigators of sin and evil, so they as well as people are without excuse. All the same, people are still culpable for sin, since they are the ones who transgress against God. With regard to how this culpability occurs, Calvin advised that "it is better not to say anything, or at least to touch upon it lightly":

> But although these things are briefly and not very clearly stated, they are more than enough to clear God's majesty of all slander. And what concern is it to us to know anything more about devils or to know it for another purpose? Some persons grumble that Scripture does not in numerous passages set forth systematically and clearly that fall of the devils, its cause, manner, time, and character. But because this has nothing to do with us, it was better not to say anything, or at least to touch upon it lightly, because it did not befit the Holy Spirit to feed our curiosity with empty histories to no effect. And we see that the Lord's purpose was to teach nothing in his sacred oracles except what we should learn to our edification. Therefore, lest we ourselves linger over superfluous matters, let us be content with this brief summary of the nature of devils: they were when first created angels of God, but by degeneration they ruined themselves, and became the instruments of ruin for others.[8]

God is not thought to be directly involved with causing sin, either among demons or people, and thus Calvin thought it wrong to believe that God is

4

in any way imaginable responsible for sin and evil. Such knowledge is not for "our edification"; if it was otherwise, then we must be content to know that God would have informed us.

From the outset of the *Institutes,* Calvin warns readers that God has not fully revealed all matters to humanity. Some truths are too great for people to understand because God and the ways of God are ineffable—that is, beyond human comprehension. He said: "Indeed, his essence is incomprehensible; hence, his divineness far escapes all human perception. But upon his individual works he has engraved unmistakable marks of his glory, so clear and so prominent that even unlettered and stupid folk cannot plead the excuse of ignorance."[9] The ways of God are hidden, and people ought not to be curious about questions asked that are not explicitly answered in the Bible. But sufficient knowledge of what people need to know is available, and most clearly available in the Bible. It is best to trust in what the Bible says, believing it reveals all that we need to know about God, and be content with the blessings it conveys. Calvin warned people against being too theologically curious. He said:

> First, then, let them remember that when they inquire into predestination they are penetrating the sacred precincts of divine wisdom. If anyone with carefree assurance breaks into this place, he will not succeed in satisfying his curiosity and he will enter a labyrinth from which he can find no exit. For it is not right for man unrestrainedly to search out things that the Lord has willed to be hid in himself, and to unfold from eternity itself the sublimest wisdom, which he would have us revere but not understand that through this also he should fill us with wonder. He has set forth by his Word the secrets of his will that he has decided to reveal to us. These he decided to reveal in so far as he foresaw that they would concern us and benefit us.[10]

More will be said about Calvin's doctrine of predestination later, but Calvin made it clear that people should restrain their curiosity. Suffice it to say that God is in control and we should free ourselves of every care since "the secrets of his will" transcend our human understanding. If people insist on questioning the goodness or works of God, then they will become lost as if in a labyrinth or maze from which there is "no exit." One ought to accept what Calvin believed were the clear teachings of the Bible about God's sovereign power to affect all the blessings promised and disregard questions and concerns about the logistics of such beliefs.

From Calvin's perspective, people should rest in their understanding of God's sovereignty, power, and majesty. Life is difficult to understand, much less live. Yet God has revealed to us in the Bible that God is in absolute control. We do not need to worry about that over which, ultimately speaking, we have no control. There is one who is in control, and we may rest in peace, knowing that God will care for us since we are unable to care for ourselves. Again, praise and thanks be to God who compensates for the apparent neediness people endure spiritually, intellectually, emotionally, relationally, and socially!

It was obvious to Calvin that people's knowledge is finite, and their utter sinfulness seemed equally obvious to him. By themselves, people possess neither the cognitive nor spiritual power to answer the questions and concerns they have, much less questions and concerns about eternal life. If anyone has sufficient power to meet all of people's questions and concerns, then it is God. In contemplating the overwhelming greatness (and direness) of people's life situation, what alternative do people have other than to submit humbly and obediently to God, the only one who conceivably has sufficient power to help finite, sinful people?

Because of the teachings of the Bible, Calvin deduced that mere human deliberation could not penetrate God's sovereignty. People ought to submit to the authority of the Bible and its clear, propositional statements about the sovereignty, majesty, and glory of God. What the Bible does not clearly state propositionally ought not to be questioned—that is, at least not at length. God has not seen fit to answer all questions and concerns that people have; yet, knowing that God, ultimately speaking, controls all there is may encourage them. We need not be concerned about trying to fathom all mysteries that exist. Instead we should trust that God, like a loving parent, knows that knowledge of all things is not good for us; and again, like a loving parent, God cares for those needs for which we cannot care for ourselves.

Christians in particular ought to affirm what the Bible says about God's sovereignty, majesty, and glory, and be overjoyed that God has elected them to salvation. Their faith is a gift, which they have not earned, since faith that people have comes from God and not from themselves. Christians would not have faith if they were not among the elect—those whom God has to receive eternal life. Thus they should give praise and thanks to God for the immeasurable blessing of eternal life, wrought through the atonement of Jesus Christ.

Wesley's View of God

Like Calvin, Wesley believed in the sovereignty of God. In "Thoughts upon God's Sovereignty," he said: "As a Creator, he has acted, in all things, according to his own sovereign will.... Here, therefore, he may, in the most absolute sense, do what he will with his own. Accordingly, he created the heavens and the earth, and all things that are therein, in every conceivable respect, 'according to his own good pleasure.'"[11] Wesley also believed in the omnipotent power of God. He said:

> And he is omnipotent, as well as omnipresent; there can be no more bounds to his power, than to his presence. He "hath a mighty arm; strong is his hand, and high is his right hand." He doeth whatsoever pleaseth him, in the heavens, the earth, the sea, and in all deep places. With men we know many things are impossible, but not with God: With him "all things are possible." Whensoever he willeth, to do is present with him.[12]

So Wesley aligned with both the Bible and historic Christianity in affirming the sovereign, almighty power of God. From Wesley's perspective, there was no question about God's ability to accomplish all that God intends to do in creation and among people.

But Wesley did not think about the sovereignty of God, except in relationship to the holiness of God. He considered holiness to be fundamental for a biblical understanding of God, and holiness involves more than power. The holiness of God distinguishes God above everyone and everything else in the world. It includes truth and justice as well as love and mercy. So people ought not to think of God primarily in terms of power because it can cause them to lose sight of God's concern to be in relationship with the people who God created. Being in relationship includes relational attributes of love, grace, patience, goodness, and forgiveness of those from whom God expects accountability. With regard to God's holiness, Wesley said:

> Holiness is another of the attributes of the almighty, all-wise God. He is infinitely distant from every touch of evil. He "is light; and in him is no darkness at all." He is a God of unblemished justice and truth; but above all is his mercy. This we may easily learn from that beautiful passage in the thirty-third and fourth chapters of Exodus: "And Moses said, I beseech thee, show me thy glory. And the Lord descended in the cloud, and proclaimed the name of the Lord,—The Lord, The Lord God, merciful and gracious, longsuffering, and abundant in goodness and truth, keeping mercy for thousands, and forgiving iniquity and transgression and sin."[13]

God's holiness, of course, is not merely a matter of God's essence or being; it is an attribute for which Christians should be concerned. Nor is God's sovereignty more important than other attributes of God, including God's love and relations with people. To be sure, the attributes of God should be understood to include the love of God and the ways in which people may grow in loving relationship with God and others.

God created people to be in relationship with God as well as others. God's sovereignty does not preclude a genuine ability (or power) on the part of people to decide whether and how to relate to God. Of course, that power is no longer natural to them because of the effects of sin. But God provides grace that enables people a sufficient amount of volitional power to respond to God's gracious overtures for salvation as well as for growth in relationship. After all, the Bible describes salvation as reconciliation—the reconciling of relationship between two (or more) persons. Salvation involves more than a change in juridical relationship; it involves a quality of mutuality, which God enables by grace. By permitting people a measure of volition, God does not become less sovereign. Indeed, Wesley thought that sovereignty implies a greater achievement, namely provision for people to choose freely to respond to God in love as well as faith and hope. To be sure, volitional power on the part of people occurs by God's grace, permitting people to choose genuinely and not determinatively.

Affirmation of the sovereignty of God does not preclude God from voluntarily restricting divine power, so to speak, so that people may exercise genuine freedom of choice, which is crucial for their relationship with God. Of course, Wesley did not think about people's free will as an innate human ability, without the aid of God's gracious providence. On the contrary, Wesley agreed with Calvin's rejection of Pelagianism and Semi-Pelagianism, which placed the initiation of salvation upon people, rather than upon God. Indeed, Christian debate over the relationship between divine predestination and human freedom long predated both Calvin and Wesley. But the debate heated up with Luther and Calvin's reintroduction of Augustine's condemnation of all forms of Pelagianism as salvation by works righteousness, which the Bible clearly rejects, especially in the writings of the Apostle Paul. Unfortunately, Calvin—like Augustine—tended to put the debate in either-or terms: either salvation is earned by human merit (Pelagianism) or unmerited by divine grace (Augustinianism). However, the debate is far more complex, and more than two views arose in church history. Just as Augustine argued against Semi-Pelagianism, which does not argue as exactingly for works righteousness as Pelagianism, there arose what could—at least—be called a Semi-Augustinian view. The Semi-Augustinian view supplanted Augustinianism in church history and continues to be the dominant view among Christians today, despite the arguments of Luther and Calvin to the contrary.

Semi-Augustinianism may be used to describe Catholic, Orthodox, and Anglican views of divine predestination and human freedom that developed in contradistinction to what was considered Augustine's authoritarian view of God's predestinarianism. Such Semi-Augustinian views may be found in historic Christian leaders such as Caesarius of Arles, Thomas Aquinas, and Desiderius Erasmus, as well as many others who lived prior to Calvin. Semi-Augustinianism affirms that God graciously initiates, sustains, and completes the salvation of people, and thus people must choose to accept or reject their salvation and reconciliation with God. God voluntarily limits divine power over people so that their decisions are not effectually determined. At minimum, people must believe or resist God's overtures for salvation. Because God eternally knows the decisions of people, God responds to them accordingly, working through the Holy Spirit to redeem everyone. To people, such divine knowledge seems like foreknowledge, but that is because of their finite understanding of time. Thus, God graciously enables people so that they have sufficient power to choose freely to accept or reject God's gift of salvation through Jesus Christ.

Divine self-limitation is not thought to represent an actual limitation in the sovereignty, power, and majesty of God. If God voluntarily chooses to permit people some genuine measure of freedom, that permission does not represent a diminution of God. In the same way, God permits the whole of creation to function with some genuine measure of freedom. For that reason, it is possible to study scientifically the laws of nature, so to speak. As such, the laws of nature function with a degree of independence from God's direct causation, just as people function with a degree of independence from God's direct causation. To be sure, God continues to care providentially for creation and for people. But the various laws of nature and activities of people may be investigated inductively, deductively, and in other ways. Indeed, great amounts of knowledge and wisdom may be accumulated in order to aid people as well as the world through scientific, technological, medical, and other disciplines. Such investigations ought not to be seen as a limitation upon God, but rather as an outflowing of the sovereignty, power, and majesty of God, who makes such investigations possible.

Wesley considered himself a faithful follower of the Anglo-Catholic tradition of Christian theology that emphasized both divine sovereignty and human freedom. If he disagreed with Calvin, it had as much to do with his fidelity to the church tradition in which he had been raised, educated, and ordained, rather than as a polemic against Calvin. To be sure, Wesley had disagreements with followers of Calvin in his day, but he did so convinced that the Anglo-Catholic tradition of Christianity better represented the teachings of the Bible than the Augustinian-Calvinist tradition of Protestantism. God does indeed predestine people, according to Wesley, but it is conditioned on God's eternal knowledge (or foreknowledge) rather than on God's divine decrees (see Romans 8:29). Accordingly, with regard to Calvinist challenges that his theology reduced the sovereignty of God, Wesley said:

> Natural free-will, in the present state of mankind, I do not understand: I only assert, that there is a measure of free-will supernaturally restored to

9

every man, together with that supernatural light which "enlightens every man that cometh into the world." But indeed, whether this be natural or no, as to your objection it matters not. For that equally lies against both, against any free-will of any kind; your assertion being thus, "If man has any free-will, God cannot have the whole glory of his salvation;" or, "It is not so much for the glory of God, to save man as a free agent, put into a capacity of concurring with his grace on the one hand, and of resisting it on the other; as to save him in the way of a necessary agent, by a power which he cannot possibly resist."[14]

From Wesley's perspective, it was absurd to think that God's sovereignty was in any way diminished by allowing people a measure of freedom and responsibility. On the contrary, he considered it far less convincing to believe in a God who ultimately precluded any human freedom, other than the freedom to do that which God had foreordained for people to think, say, and do.

In talking about the sovereignty of God, Wesley distinguished between God's work as creator of the world and as governor of the world. As creator, God acted in all things according to God's sovereign will; as judge, God governs people who were created in the image of God, who have a measure of freedom like God has freedom, since they were created in the image of God. Of course, God's freedom is infinite, while people's freedom is finite, and there are many factors—spiritual, physical, emotional, and cultural—that diminish human free will. But it is genuine freedom nonetheless, and God governs the world filled with people who are expected to act responsibly. Wesley said, "Of his own good pleasure, he made such a creature as man, an embodied spirit, and, in consequence of his spiritual nature, endued with understanding, will, and liberty."[15] God created people to exercise understanding, will, and liberty—that is, freedom—but God does not irresistibly determine such exercises. Instead, God graciously creates and sustains people with the potential to choose, including the potential to sin, but never leaves them without the option for redemption.

Love of God

The more Wesley interacted with the followers of Calvin, the less patience he had with their beliefs, which he considered mistaken with regard both to how they viewed God and how they viewed the Christian life. For Wesley, it largely had to do with his understanding of God as loving. He was profoundly influenced by how God's love must predominate how we view God and God's relationship with us. For example, 1 John 4:7-12 says:

> Beloved, let us love one another, because love is from God; everyone who loves is born of God and knows God. Whoever does not love does not know

God, for God is love. God's love was revealed among us in this way: God sent his only Son into the world so that we might live through him. In this is love, not that we loved God but that he loved us and sent his Son to be the atoning sacrifice for our sins. Beloved, since God loved us so much, we also ought to love one another. No one has ever seen God; if we love one another, God lives in us, and his love is perfected in us.

Here the Bible says that "God is love," and Wesley thought that the crucial message of the Bible has more to do with uplifting the love of God than the power of God—not that the power of God's sovereignty is unimportant, but that power without love misses out on the full self-revelation of God to people in the Bible. In fact, in commentary on 1 John 4:8 above, Wesley described love as God's "darling, his reigning attribute, the attribute that sheds an amiable glory on all his other perfections."[16]

Of course, Calvin spoke about the love of God. For example, he said, "Indeed, no one gives himself freely and willingly to God's service unless, having tasted his fatherly love, he is drawn to love and worship him in return."[17] Calvin continued by saying that the work of the atonement derives from God's love. He said:

> For this reason, Paul says that the love with which God embraced us "before the creation of the world" was established and grounded in Christ [Eph. 1:4-5]. These things are plain and in agreement with Scripture, and beautifully harmonize those passages in which it is said that God declared his love toward us in giving his only-begotten Son to die [John 3:16]; and, conversely, that God was our enemy before he was again made favorable to us by Christ's death [Rom. 5:10].[18]

So love definitely factors into Calvin's theology, but it is not the primary focus. A brief perusal of book headings in the *Institutes* reveals a stronger emphasis on God as creator, on knowledge of God, on law and gospel, on the benefits and effects of grace, and on the church. Themes found in Calvin's chapters include the Bible, the power of God, the secret working of the Spirit, faith, eternal election, and so on. But love does not explicitly appear in the content headings of the *Institutes*. Even in the substance of Calvin's writings, love is not a prominent theme—at least not as prominent as Wesley wanted.

One of the reasons Wesley emphasized the dynamic nature of God's love so much had to do with his relational view of the Trinity—of three persons in loving relationship within God. For the most part, he did not query much about the mysteries of the triune nature of God the Father, Son, and Holy Spirit. Still, Wesley envisioned the "new creation" to come as "a constant communion with the Father and his Son Jesus Christ, through the Spirit; a continual enjoyment of the Three-One God, and of all the creatures in him."[19] Although Wesley did not focus at length on the doctrine of the Trinity, he was appalled that Calvin promoted the execution of the Spaniard Servetus in part because of an unorthodox view of the Trinity. Wesley said: "I think them very good words [i.e., Trinity and Person]. But I should think it very hard to be burned alive for not using them; especially with a slow fire, made of moist, green wood!"[20]

According to Wesley, divine sovereignty and love are not contradictory; they are complementary. Of course, a similar argument could be made in description of Calvin, since he talked about God's love as well as God's sovereignty. Yet, Calvin emphasized sovereignty far more than he emphasized love. Wesley, however, said that it is because of God's sovereign, holy love that God created people in God's own image, providentially cares for them even when they do not return love to God, and provides for their redemption so that they willingly—and not by divine compulsion—love. Of God's love, Wesley said:

> If God *SO* loved us;—observe, the stress of the argument lies on this very point: *SO loved us*, as to deliver up his only Son to die a cursed death for our salvation. Beloved, what manner of love is this wherewith God hath loved us; so as to give his *only Son*, in glory equal with the Father, in Majesty co-eternal? What manner of love is this wherewith the only-begotten Son of God hath loved us so as to *empty himself*, as far as possible, of his eternal Godhead; as to divest himself of that glory which he had with the Father before the world began; as to take upon him the form of a servant.[21]

Reference to Jesus as having emptied himself of his divine prerogatives exemplifies the voluntary as well as loving nature of God's relationship with people. Just as God voluntarily limited divine control over people in order that they might exercise freedom to choose and freedom to love, the Son of God, Jesus, voluntarily acted to redeem people from their abuses of freedom—that is, from their sin.

In contrast to Calvin and his followers, Wesley said that God's loving-kindness must be maintained as primary in understanding all the other attributes of God. He said:

> So ill do election and reprobation agree with the truth and sincerity of God! But do they not agree least of all with the scriptural account of his love and goodness? that attribute which God peculiarly claims, wherein he glories above all the rest. It is not written, "God is justice," or "God is truth:" (Although he is just and true in all his ways:) But it is written, "God is love," love in the abstract, without bounds; and "there is no end of his goodness." His love extends even to those who neither love nor fear him. He is good, even to the evil and the unthankful; yea, without any exception or limita-

12

tion, to all the children of men. For "the Lord is loving" (or good) "to every man, and his mercy is over all his works."[22]

Wesley was particularly concerned about how the followers of Calvin placed the sovereignty and power of God over the holiness and love of God. He asked:

> But how is God good or loving to a reprobate, or one that is not elected? (You may choose either term: For if none but the unconditionally elect are saved, it comes precisely to the same thing.) You cannot say, he is an object of the love or goodness of God, with regard to his eternal state, whom he created, says Mr. Calvin plainly and fairly, *in vitae contumeliam et mortis exitium,* "to live a reproach, and die everlastingly."[23]

In Wesley's opinion, Calvin's doctrine of God, especially as it pertains to God's role in people's election and reprobation, "is a doctrine of blasphemy"; it makes God "more cruel, more false, and unjust than the devil."[24]

Perhaps Charles Wesley, John's brother, provides the *pièce de résistance* with regard to the Wesleys' disagreement with the theology of Calvin and his followers. Charles was a poet and hymnist for the Methodist movement, and he wrote *Hymns on God's Everlasting Love.* In this collection he wrote hymnody contrasting Calvin's "horrible decree" with the Wesleys' "decree of love." Consider the following hymn that Charles wrote on "free grace":

> We need no reprobates to prove
> That grace, free-grace is truly free,
> Who cannot see that God is love,
> Open your eyes, and look on me,
>
> On us, whom Jesus hath call'd forth,
> T' assert that all his grace may have,
> To vindicate his passion's worth
> Enough ten thousand worlds to save.
>
> He made it possible for all
> His gift of righteousness t'embrace,
> We all may answer to his call,
>
> May all be freely sav'd by grace.
> He promis'd all mankind to draw;
> We feel him draw us from above;
> And preach with him the gracious law,
> And publish the DECREE OF LOVE.[25]

Importance of Our Views of God

How we view God is inextricably bound up with how we, in turn, think about ourselves and the world in which we live—what we say and what we do. It affects our relationship with God as well as our understanding of God. Our view of God influences whether we are hopeful about the future or whether we are resigned to forces beyond our control. It influences how responsive or diffident we are to circumstances. Do we think of ourselves as active participants in the world, spiritually as well as physically? Although we must ultimately trust in God for how life unfolds, to what degree do we believe that God wants us to be active participants?

A Calvinist, of course, would disagree with Wesley's assessment of divine predestination and human freedom. Based upon God's sovereign control, Christians may be hopeful and responsive, not Stoic, which Calvin critiqued as a godless philosophy. Calvin would argue that any theologies that allow for human freedom, however they are conceived, run the risk of Pelagianism— that is, the usurpation of God's sovereignty for the imagined exercise of people's role in their eternal as well as earthly well-being. As we will see, Calvin allows for a type of human freedom compatible with divine sovereignty, but his view of freedom ultimately cannot resist God's grace. Thus, any theology that takes on responsibilities that God never intended for people to have, Calvin would argue, errs on the side of transgressing the first of the Ten Commandments, which dishonors God's glory and majesty.

Just as Calvin would have thought that Wesley was wrong, Wesley considered Calvin to be wrong. From Wesley's perspective, God needs to be viewed with more love than power; more relationally than regally; more self-giving (and self-limiting) than authoritarian. To be sure, there are verses in the Bible that seem to affirm Calvin's view of God, and such verses ought not to be dismissed. Neither should other verses, which Wesley pointed out, be dismissed that establish love as decisive in best conceptualizing the person and works of God. Although biblical passages affirm the sovereign power of God, those passages do not suggest an authoritarianism that precludes freely chosen relationships and love on the part of people, especially in their relations with God.

Philip Schaff may best sum up Wesley's critique of Calvin with regard to his understanding of God. Schaff was from the German Reformed tradition, and became an internationally known church historian at the turn of the twentieth century. Of Calvin and those who followed him, Schaff said:

> The Calvinistic system is popularly (though not quite correctly) identified
> with the Augustinian system, and shares its merit...but also its fundamen-

tal defect of confining the saving grace of God and the atoning work of Christ to a small circle of the elect, and ignoring the general love of God to all mankind (John 3:16). It is a theology of Divine sovereignty rather than Divine love.[26]

Final Thoughts

Both Wesley and Calvin believed in the sovereignty, power, and majesty of God. Calvin thought that such beliefs resulted in divine control of all that happens, and that people ought to praise and give thanks to God for all that happens. Wesley thought that such beliefs resulted in divine control, which God limited for the sake of people who might exercise freedom—by the grace of God—to accept God's salvation and to love God in return. Wesley thought that Calvin was mistaken to believe that God's sovereignty so overwhelms the freedom of people as to make it negligible or nonexistent.

Most Christians believe that God is sovereign and that they have a significant amount of freedom, both with regard to repenting and believing in God for their salvation, and for day-to-day decisions they make. Their sense of freedom to make significant decisions for this life and for their eternal life is not illusory. Although their decision making is made possible by God's grace, they too give praise and thanks to God's Spirit for aiding them in all that happens. Because of this grace-enabled liberty, Christians may also love as they are loved by God. In the words of John, "We love because he first loved us" (1 John 4:19).

Discussion Questions

1. In what ways would you say that Wesley and Calvin most agree and disagree about how they view God?

2. What is important about the sovereignty of God—of God's almighty power?

3. Given the sovereignty of God, to what degree do you think that people are free to decide about their salvation or about other aspects of their lives?

4. What is important about the love of God—of God's goodness and grace toward people?

5. What are other important attributes of God?

6. Why is it important for Christians to think about their view of God and about how it affects their lives?

BIBLE: MORE PRIMARY THAN SOLE AUTHORITY

All scripture is inspired by God and is useful for teaching, for reproof, for correction, and for training in righteousness, so that everyone who belongs to God may be proficient, equipped for every good work. (2 Timothy 3:16-17)

When I teach courses in Christian theology, students sometimes find it difficult to explain what they believe about particular doctrinal issues. Or, in some instances, they can recite what they have been taught about Christian doctrine, but they do not really know what it means. In such cases, I may ask students not what they believe, but how they live. For example, with regard to the Bible, students may self-confidently claim that the Bible is the word of God: it is inspired, authoritative, and truthful. They may not be able to explain what divine inspiration, religious authority, and biblical truth mean precisely, but they earnestly assert them nonetheless.

In response, I ask students not what they believe about the Bible, but how it actually functions in their lives. For example, how often do they read the Bible? Once a day? Once a week? Once a month? For all the confessional statements students may make about the excellences of the Bible, their actions may not substantiate their faith claims if they only read the Bible once per week. In such instances, their statements of belief do not really match their words. In fact, one could argue that they consider the Bible to be rather unimportant and perhaps expendable on a day-to-day basis. Despite students' exemplary theological affirmations about the Bible, such statements seem hollow if their actions (practice) do not support their beliefs (theory).

What about decision making? To what degree does the Bible factor into students' decision making? Perhaps with regard to especially mysterious doctrines, like the Trinity and the Incarnation, the Bible represents the only pertinent authority for their doctrinal beliefs. But what about everyday life decisions such as how to spend their time, labor, and money? What about values used to decide what television programs and movies to watch, what cars and houses to buy, or what political policies and candidates to support? As important as students may claim the Bible is for their lives, does it really factor into their decision making or only when it is convenient—if ever?

Wesley and Calvin held similar views about the Bible, and both used it daily in how they lived, taught, and gave leadership. They shared many similarities in their views about the divine inspiration, authority, and truthfulness of the Bible; so, not much time will be spent in comparing how they viewed the Bible per se. But there were differences in how they understood and promoted the Bible in their respective theologies and ministries. In particular, consider the following question: Does the Bible stand alone as religiously authoritative, or does a more dynamic relationship exist between the Bible and other factors in Christian decision making?

At first glance, the differences between Wesley and Calvin may not seem significant. Complicating matters, however, are those who followed both Wesley and Calvin—sometimes overemphasizing things Wesley and Calvin said, while underemphasizing other things. To be sure, clear differences occurred between how Wesley and Calvin viewed the Bible, relative to other factors or religious authorities. These differences are not only important for understanding their respective views of the Bible; they are also important for understanding differences between how Wesley and Calvin viewed other aspects of Christianity, for example, how they viewed salvation, the church, and ministry.

Calvin's View of the Bible

Calvin began the *Institutes* by talking about God in the first five chapters, and he continued by talking about the Bible in the next five chapters. Calvin used the term *Scripture,* rather than the *Bible*. Historically, Scripture (or Scriptures) means "writing, or writings," and Bible means "book, or books." Holy Scripture (or Sacred Scripture) and Holy Bible are Christian ways of referring to the canon (or standard) of writings considered to be holy, sacred, and divinely inspired by God, as described in 2 Timothy 3:16-17: "All scripture is inspired by God and is useful for teaching, for reproof, for correction, and for training in righteousness, so that everyone who belongs to God may be proficient, equipped for every good work." Usually Christians refer to either Scripture or the Bible. In this book, I use the two terms synonymously.

In the *Institutes,* Calvin stated that the Bible is needed to teach and guide those who believe in God, who is the sovereign creator and redeemer. The Bible functions like "spectacles" (or reading glasses), which aids people in knowing God. Calvin said:

> Just as old bleary-eyed men and those with weak vision, if you thrust before them a most beautiful volume, even if they recognize it to be some sort of writing, yet can scarcely construe two words, but with the aid of spectacles will begin to read distinctly; so Scripture, gathering up the otherwise confused knowledge of God in our minds, having dispersed our dullness, clearly shows us the true God.[1]

The Bible is especially needed for salvation, since people cannot know about it without divine revelation.

Calvin considered the Bible to be inspired by the Holy Spirit, and its certain authority is confirmed by the witness of the Holy Spirit and not by any other authorization. Here Calvin distinguished his view of the Bible from Roman Catholicism, since the latter considered the Bible to be part of a broader understanding of church authority that included the canonization process of the Bible. Although Catholics believe that the Bible is divinely inspired, God's Holy Spirit worked through the leadership, councils, and decisions of the church to canonize its contents. Thus the Catholic Church has priority over biblical authority both historically and theologically, since it was the ancient church that codified the Bible. However, Calvin disagreed, saying that God alone, through the Holy Spirit, testifies to the inspiration, authority, and truthfulness of the Bible, and not by any human or church authorization. He said:

> Let this point therefore stand: that those whom the Holy Spirit has inwardly taught truly rest upon Scripture, and that Scripture indeed is self-authenticated; hence, it is not right to subject it to proof and reasoning. And the certainty it deserves with us, it attains by the testimony of the Spirit....Therefore, illumined by his power, we believe neither by our own nor by anyone else's judgment that Scripture is from God; but above human judgment we affirm with utter certainty.[2]

Calvin argued that it is the church that is based on the Bible, and not vice versa. To the degree that the church attests to the Bible, it speaks truthfully and authoritatively. As such, the church does not represent authority to authorize the Bible, since the church's authority is derived from it.

Although Calvin appealed primarily to the "secret testimony of the Holy Spirit" to establish the divine inspiration, authority, and truthfulness of the Bible, he argued that human reason—though limited—provides sufficiently firm proofs to establish the Bible's credibility.[3] The simplicity of biblical truths, including its order and inner harmony, corroborates its inspiration, authority, and truthfulness.[4]

With regard to biblical interpretation, Calvin was proficient in his approach to hermeneutics—the study of the theory and practice of biblical interpretation. After all, he wrote commentaries on most of the books of the Bible. Of course, Calvin lived long before the nineteenth-century rise of historical criticism, so it is anachronistic to speculate about Calvin's hermeneutics in comparison to later developments. He was certainly aware of biblical interpretive practices from the ancient and medieval churches as well as the contemporary hermeneutics of Luther, Erasmus, Philipp Melanchthon, and Martin Bucer. Calvin knew about the fourfold methodology—the *Quadriga*—that sought after the literal (historical), allegorical (symbolic), topological (moral), and anagogical (metaphysical, or eschatological) senses of the Bible. According to Raymond Blacketer, Calvin focused on "what he calls the *sens naturel,* the literal, historical, straightforward meaning of the text. In comparison with other exegetes of his day, Calvin is less apt to engage in speculative exegesis, and he frequently criticizes the method of finding multiple spiritual senses in the text, such as characterized medieval interpretation, embodied in what is known as the Quadriga."[5]

Although wide-ranging in his study of the Bible, Calvin avoided protracted, convoluted, and speculative debate over biblical interpretation. He wrote straightforward commentaries because he thought that people were capable of studying the Bible for themselves. Calvin agreed with Luther's ideas about the perspicacity of the Bible, namely, that it is not too difficult or mysterious for people to read and understand by themselves. The church and biblical scholars may aid people in reading and understanding the Bible, but individuals have sufficient wherewithal to read, understand, and interpret it.

Calvin was concerned about critiquing what he considered to be superstitious and sometimes fanatical approaches to Christianity, for example, when people claimed present-day prophecies from God. His concern was, in part, because of ongoing claims by Roman Catholics that God continues to speak through the pope and the Catholic magisterium, which represents the teaching authority of the pope and the college of bishops, rather than through the Bible. He rejected the authority of the pope and the Catholic magisterium. Calvin also rejected those who claimed new revelation from the Holy Spirit today that exceeds biblical teachings, which he thought occurred among many Anabaptists. According to Calvin, God's Spirit does not lead us beyond the Bible. It is the safeguard against revelatory claims to extrabiblical revelation, whether prophetic claims come through the church or individuals. Calvin said: "Therefore the Spirit, promised to us, has not the task of inventing new and unheard-of revelations, or of forging a new kind of doctrine, to lead us away from the received doctrine of the gospel, but of sealing our minds with that very doctrine which is commended by the gospel."[6]

Calvin and *Sola Scriptura*

Like Luther, Calvin argued for the authority of the Bible in determining Christian beliefs, values, and practices. In this regard, he embodied the Reformation slogan of *sola Scriptura* (Latin, "Scripture alone"). Interestingly, Calvin did not use this precise phraseology in the *Institutes*. However, the substance of *sola Scriptura* can be found throughout his writings. Luther, however, overtly defended himself in a heresy trial at the 1521 Diet of Worms with the following words:

> If I do not become convinced by the testimony of Scripture or clear rational grounds—for I believe neither the pope nor councils alone, since it is obvious that they have erred on several occasions—I remain subjugated by the scriptural passages I have cited and my conscience held captive by the word of God. Therefore, I neither can nor will recant anything. For to act against conscience is difficult, noxious, and dangerous. May God help me. Amen.[7]

After making this confession, Luther is thought to have said, "Here I stand! I cannot do otherwise," though historians consider these words an early legendary addition.[8] Be that as it may, the quotation above reflects the staunch stand that Luther took in confronting the papal and magisterial authority of the Roman Catholic Church, displacing it with the authority of the Bible. Although Luther utilized "clear rational grounds" and "conscience" in his defense, the authority to which he appealed was Scripture alone. Thus *sola Scriptura* has often been described as the formal principle or cause (that is, authoritative source) of the Reformation, since Luther and other reformers established the Bible as their normative religious authority.

The principle of *sola Scriptura* is present throughout the writings of Calvin. In talking about true religion, Calvin said, "Now, in order that true religion may shine upon us, we ought to hold that it must take its beginning from heavenly doctrine and that no one can get even the slightest taste of right and sound doctrine unless he be a pupil of Scripture."[9] Because of the effects of sin, human authority and even church authority must not be equated with the authority of the Bible. Instead Calvin clearly emphasized the Bible as the prescriptive standard of Christianity. He said: "Let this be a firm principle: No other word is to be held as the Word of God, and given place as such in the church, than what is contained first in the Law and the Prophets, then in the writings of the apostles; and the only authorized way of teaching in the church is by the prescription and standard of his Word."[10]

Calvin was not woodenly or uncritically literalistic in his understanding of biblical authority. He was remarkably sophisticated in understanding that, secondary to the Bible, Christians need to employ historical Christian teachings, especially from the most ancient patristic writers, as well as critical thinking in theological decision making. This sophistication was sometimes lost upon Protestants during the Reformation, for example, Anabaptists who unrelentingly appealed to no authority other than the Bible. It was also sometimes lost upon later Protestants who thought that *sola Scriptura* meant that absolutely no other resources or factors had any legitimate input. Even today, Christians may naively argue that the Bible only—and nothing else—should inform their beliefs, values, and practices. However, even a cursory look at the decision making of such people reveals that they commonly rely upon doctrinal developments from church history, logical argumentation, and obvious experiential confirmation for their most cherished beliefs, values, and practices, though without acknowledgment.

Calvin was concerned that the Reformation not be considered something new, and especially not heretical; he makes this clear in the preface to the *Institutes*. Instead, Calvin argued that Protestantism was in continuity with both the Bible and Christian antiquity—a continuity that he thought Roman Catholicism distorted. Throughout Calvin's writings, references can be found to such patristic writers as Jerome, Augustine, and Chrysostom as Christian authorities to whom Calvin appealed in developing his theology and ministry. He drew upon the writings of Augustine the most, especially when talking about the relationship between divine predestination and human freedom. Finally, Calvin helped oversee the creation of Protestant ordinances and confessions that, along with the Bible and his own writings, became foundational for his followers.

Wesley's View of the Bible

Wesley was a lover of the Bible. He believed in its divine inspiration, religious authority, and truthfulness, just as did Calvin. In the preface to his *Sermons,* Wesley talked about the importance of the Bible, especially for the sake of salvation, and he famously described himself as *homo unius libri* (Latin, "a man of one book"): "I want to know one thing, the way to heaven—how to land safe on that happy shore. God himself has condescended to teach the way: for this very end he came from heaven. He hath written it down in a book. O give me that book! At any price give me the Book of God! I have it. Here is knowledge enough for me. Let me be *homo unius libri.*"[11] Wesley agreed with Protestants in their focus upon the primacy of scriptural authority in matters of faith and practice. Although he lived two centuries after the Reformation, conflict between Protestants and Roman Catholics continued, and Wesley affirmed "the written word of God to be the only and sufficient rule both of Christian faith and practice; and herein we are fundamentally distinguished from those of the Romish Church."[12]

Wesley believed that the Holy Spirit inspired the writing, canonization, and transmission of the Bible and that today the Holy Spirit chooses principally to guide people through it. He said: "For though the Spirit is our principal leader, yet He is not our rule at all; the Scriptures are the rule whereby He leads us into all truth. Therefore, only talk good English, call the Spirit our 'guide,' which signifies an intelligent being, and the Scriptures our 'rule,' which signifies something used by an intelligent being, and all is plain and clear."[13] So the Bible is guaranteed by the Holy Spirit and also by rational and empirical evidences, since it comes through an intelligent creator. Thus, in talking about the inspiration of the Bible, Wesley appealed to "four grand and powerful arguments which strongly induce us to believe that the Bible must be from God; viz., miracles, prophecies, the goodness of the doctrine, and the moral character of the penmen."[14]

Although Wesley had a high view of the Bible, he was not simplistically a man of one book. On the contrary, Wesley was an Oxford University tutor who was well aware of church history, including its ecclesiastical and theological developments. He read, edited, and wrote vast numbers of books, and required that the pastors and lay leaders he supervised read widely from classics of Western civilization, logic, and rhetoric as well as the Bible in preparing them to provide leadership in churches and ministry. In his "Minutes of Several Conversations," Wesley responded to Methodist leaders who argued that they only needed to study the Bible: "This is rank enthusiasm. If you need no book but the Bible, you are got above St. Paul. He wanted others too. 'Bring the books,' says he, 'but especially the parchments,' those wrote on parchment. 'But I have no taste for reading.' Contract a taste for it by use, or return to your trade."[15] Wesley understood that theology, spirituality, and ministry are not narrow disciplines, isolated from a rich context of learning from multiple sources beyond the person and work of the Holy Spirit in people's lives as well as the Bible.

For example, Wesley viewed himself firmly within the context of the Anglo-Catholic tradition of Protestantism. He was a lifelong ordained minister in the Church of England, and his theological roots were formed in its tutelage. Wesley admired and drew from the Continental reformers, but it was the British reformers with whom he most identified. Going back to

Thomas Cranmer, Wesley was part of the British Reformation in England, whose leaders considered themselves to be a *via media* (Latin, "middle way") between Roman Catholic and the Continental reformers. As such, Anglicans drank more deeply from the fountains of church tradition, including Roman Catholicism and Orthodox churches, than did Luther and Calvin. The Bible was considered the primary religious authority, but church tradition was also considered a genuine—albeit secondary—religious authority. How ought Christians to decide between the teachings of the Bible and church tradition, when they seem at odds with one another?

Anglicans believe that reason represents the God-given religious authority to discern between the Bible and church tradition, and through the dynamic interdependence of these two things, Christians can more ably discern the will of God and the Holy Spirit in matters of religion. Henry McAdoo described this methodological approach to Christianity as a way for British reformers to avoid the authoritarianism of Roman Catholicism, on the one hand, and on the other hand, to avoid uncontrolled liberty that resulted from the Continental reformers' belief in the ability of individuals to interpret the Bible for themselves. McAdoo says:

> An over-all characteristic of Anglican theological method is then this polarity or quality of living in tension, which goes far towards explaining how the element of reason did not for the most part become over-weighted during the seventeenth century since it never existed in a vacuum, theologically speaking, but operated in conjunction with other elements such as the appeal to Scripture and antiquity.[16]

The Anglican emphasis upon the primacy of religious authority, coupled with the legitimate secondary authorities of tradition and reason, did not appeal to the Continental reformers, with their preeminent focus on *sola Scriptura*.

Anglicanism arose within the context of the burgeoning Enlightenment, and such intellectual influences need to be considered when critically evaluating Wesley and his view of particular theological issues. Wesley highly valued rationality, for example, when considering the Bible, theology, and ministry. For that matter, the Continental Reformation arose within the context of humanist and nominalist ideas prevalent in the education of both Luther and Calvin, which influenced their theology. It is naive to think that Luther and Calvin developed their beliefs, values, and practices based upon the Bible alone. Both were sophisticated Christian thinkers who drew upon contemporary as well as historic rationality. Although such considerations are crucial in contextually understanding the different theological traditions of Protestantism, they cannot be reduced to them. Even so, such considerations aid us in understanding both Wesley and Calvin.

Wesley and the *Via Media*

Wesley embraced the *via media* of the Church of England, emphasizing the priority of the Bible while utilizing church tradition and critical thinking in his theology and ministry. He did not consider this to be in opposition to the Continental Reformation principle of *sola Scriptura*. On the contrary, Wesley did not interpret either Luther or Calvin as slavishly attending to the Bible only, without responsible theological and ecclesiastical dialogue with other religious authorities. He considered *sola Scriptura* to be more confirmation of the Bible as the final authority in religious matters—as the primary rather than sole authority in matters of Christian faith and practice.

Wesley referred to more than the Bible as authoritative in his theology and ministry while always maintaining the Bible as the final authority. For example, in the 1771 edition of his collected *Works,* Wesley said, "[I]n this edition I present to serious and candid men my last and Matures thoughts, agreeable, I hope, to Scripture, reason, and Christian antiquity."[17] He thought that "Christian antiquity" represented "the religion of the primitive church, of the whole church in the purest ages."[18] To be sure, Wesley did not value all church tradition equally. He valued Protestantism over Roman Catholicism, the British Reformation in England over the Continental Reformation, and the ancient church over its medieval developments. But much was to be learned from such historic authorities as well as what could be understood through logical, critical thinking.

Reason, after all, did not so much represent an intuitive source of knowledge as it served as a tool of logic and critical thinking for rightly understanding and applying Christian beliefs, values, and practices. In talking about the importance of logic, Wesley said: "For what is this, if rightly understood, but the art of good sense? of apprehending things clearly, judging truly, and reasoning conclusively?"[19] Of course, reason and rationality represent a gift from God, given by God in creation, since people are created in God's image. Certainly the finitude of humanity as well as its sinfulness requires that people faithfully discern the nature and extent of reason. Still, Wesley was sufficiently confident in the God-given gift of reason to say: "It is a fundamental principle with us [i.e., Methodists] that to renounce reason is to renounce religion, that religion and reason go hand in hand, and that all irrational religion is false religion."[20]

Although Wesley did not try to be theologically innovative, he made a noteworthy contribution to the intellectual development of Christianity when he talked about experience as a genuine religious authority alongside tradition and reason. Again, like Calvin, Wesley did not intend to create something new but to restore what had been believed throughout church history, from the time of Jesus Christ. By appealing to experiential authority, Wesley thought he was making explicit what had always been believed, valued, and practiced, though not necessarily in a conscious way, namely, that the gospel makes a verifiable difference day to day in our lives and in our world. In the preface to his *Sermons,* Wesley claimed to present "the true, the scriptural, experimental religion," reflective of "religion of the heart":

> I have endeavored to describe the true, the scriptural, experimental religion, so as to omit nothing which is a real part thereof, and to add nothing thereto which is not. And herein it is more especially my desire, first, to guard those who are just setting their faces toward heaven (and who, having little acquaintance with the things of God, are the more liable to be turned out of the way) from formality, from mere outside religion, which has almost driven heart-religion out of the world; and secondly, to warn those who know the religion of the heart, the faith which worketh by love, lest at any time they make void the law through faith, and so fall back into the snare of the devil.[21]

By experimental religion, Wesley meant the experience of God and of God's salvation, which had to do with faith and hope, but also with love experienced by believers. They sensed God's love, and they tangibly expressed love in return as well, to others. For Wesley, the reality of God and our salvation were tangible, sensed realities and not merely propositional Affirmation of the Bible. Wesley was so convinced of the experiential dimension of religious authority that he talked about how feelings matter, no matter how mercurial and difficult to discern they may be. He said:

> From these [i.e., biblical] passages it may sufficiently appear for what purpose every Christian, according to the doctrine of the Church of England, does not "receive the Holy Ghost." But this will be still more clear from those that follow; wherein the reader may likewise observe a plain, rational sense of God's revealing himself to us, of the *inspiration* of the Holy Ghost, and of a believer's *feeling* in himself the mighty working of the Spirit of Christ.[22]

Wesley was especially concerned about the felt presence of the Holy Spirit—that is, of the testimony or witness of the Holy Spirit. Calvin talked about the testimony of the Holy Spirit primarily in terms of the validity of the Bible, but Wesley thought that the experiential validation of the presence and work of the Holy Spirit in other dimensions of Christian life were also important and valid confirmations of divine truth. Christianity is more than a biblical, doctrinal, and propositional existence; it is Spirit-filled, relational, and dynamic. Wesley believed that experience represents a genuine—albeit secondary—religious authority alongside tradition and reason, relative to the primary authority of the Bible.

The Wesleyan Quadrilateral

Wesley's use of Scripture, tradition, reason, and experience has sometimes been referred to as the "Wesleyan quadrilateral." Wesley, of course, did not use the phrase, just as Calvin did not write about *sola Scriptura*. Nevertheless, both terms have become affiliated with the aforementioned men. Albert Outler coined the quadrilateral. He drew the imagery from the Lambeth Quadrilateral used by the Anglicans, which refers to four walls of a fortress that defend those inside. About the quadrilateral, Outler said:

> It was intended as a metaphor for a four-element syndrome, including the four-fold guidelines of authority in Wesley's theological method. In such a quaternity Holy Scripture is clearly unique. But this in turn is illuminated by the collective Christian wisdom of other ages and cultures between the Apostolic Age and our own. It also allows for the rescue of the Gospel from obscurantism by means of the disciplines of critical reason. But always, Biblical revelation must be received in the heart by faith: this is the requirement of "experience."[23]

Some have criticized the quadrilateral as a myth; if so, then it is a useful myth—concept, paradigm, or heuristic tool—for capturing the interdisciplinary and interdependent way that Christians reflect upon, decide, and act with regard to their heartfelt beliefs and values. One could equally say that *sola Scriptura,* for Calvin, was a myth, since he did not use the phrase; yet it is a useful one for capturing his preeminent focus upon the authority of the Bible. To be sure, the views that Wesley and Calvin had about the Bible, canon, and hermeneutics as well as religious authority are more intricate and interactive than what can simply be said. But the quadrilateral and *sola Scriptura* help us distinguish between the theological and methodological views of the two men.[24]

Although Wesley would not disagree with the *sola Scriptura* emphasis of Calvin, he would consider it inadequate to deal with the complexities of Christian beliefs and values, and especially for ministering to the real-life issues that plague people day to day. Wesley would want Christians to reflect theologically in broader ways; to consider more explicitly historic contributions that individuals, churches, and other confessional statements make; and to integrate them critically, contextually, and experimentally in life. Especially because of Wesley's emphasis upon the ongoing presence and work of the Holy Spirit, a more holistic approach to religious authority is necessary in order to comprehend the Spirit's immanent presence, interactive relationship with people, and gracious empowerment of them.

Wesley thought that the Bible is not so much solitary in its religious authority as it is primary. Of course, both Wesley and Calvin would say that, ultimately speaking, it is God who is our authority. But God has chosen to reveal a witness for how people ought to live. That witness primarily exists in the written words of God—of the Bible. To it, Christians may add other genuine —albeit secondary—religious authorities. They do not necessarily need to be talked about in terms of tradition, reason, and experience; they may also be talked about as creation, culture, or some other contextual categories. Yet Wesley provided his own helpful and insightful categories of Scripture, tradition, reason, and experience, which today carry the weight of longstanding Methodist tradition. The fourfold principle of the quadrilateral has been extremely useful. It helps in responding both to the complexities of Christian understanding and to its application to the ever-changing needs and demands of life: individually and socially; physically and spiritually; ecclesiastically and ministerially.

Let me quote from a book that I wrote on the Wesleyan quadrilateral. I talk about the value of how Wesley advocated a "living faith" more than a "systematic whole," characteristic of Calvin:

> The Wesleyan quadrilateral does not emphasize the quality of the end product so much as the quality of the approach or the means to achieve the end product. From Wesley's perspective, theology involved more of a means of addressing religious issues than a part of the end—an intricate, systematic whole. Wholeness came through process rather than completion. The quadrilateral may have dogmatic (positive) and apologetic (negative) functions, but the emphasis tends to land less on the doctrinal aspects than on living faith.[25]

Final Thoughts

Both Wesley and Calvin believed in the ultimate authority of God. Both further believed that the Bible is inspired, authoritative, and truthful. In particular, they considered the Bible to be the primary authority to which we should turn in determining matters of Christian life and faith. Calvin as well as Wesley studied and appealed preeminently to the Bible in their theological reflection so much so that Calvin is identified with the Reformation slogan of *sola Scriptura*—"Scripture alone."

Although Wesley agreed with the primacy of biblical authority, he was more explicit in appealing to other authorities as being genuine—albeit secondary—in theological reflection. He saw himself as part of the *via media*, which steered between the Continental Reformation and the theological excesses of Roman Catholicism. Wesley valued the traditions of church history, which canonized the Bible as well as passed on orthodox Christian beliefs. He valued critical thinking and the need for persuasive argumentation and preaching. Finally, Wesley valued relevant experience that confirmed biblical Christianity as well as the ongoing presence and work of the Holy Spirit in the lives of people.

Discussion Questions

1. In what ways would you say that Wesley and Calvin most agree and disagree about the Bible?

2. What do you think about the Reformation principle of *sola Scriptura*—"Scripture alone"?

3. What do you think about the prospect of more than the Bible having authoritative input into your beliefs, values, and practices?

4. Is there a difference between what you say you believe about the nature and authority of the Bible and how the Bible practically functions in your day-to-day life?

5. What do you think about Wesley's emphasis on the primacy of biblical authority, coupled with the genuine—albeit secondary—religious authority of church tradition, critical thinking, and relevant experience?

6. How is the Wesleyan quadrilateral a useful concept for thinking about the dynamic ways in which Christians make theological decisions about what they think, say, and do?

HUMANITY: MORE FREEDOM THAN PREDESTINATION

So God created humankind in his image, in the image of God he created them;
male and female he created them. (Genesis 1:27)

When I was a graduate student, a friend of mine and his wife had their first child, a son. When I visited my friend the following week, his newborn son began to cry; soon his son began to wail. My friend self-assuredly declared, "There's evidence of original sin. He wants what he wants when he wants it!" I did not quite agree with my friend, and suggested that, since his son could not yet speak, crying and indeed wailing were the only ways of communicating. But my friend disagreed. To him, his infant son's actions were proof-positive of how people are in bondage to sin, totally depraved, whether they are conscious of it or not.

I was not a parent at the time of this conversation with my friend; I now have three daughters, who have grown to adulthood. However, when my daughters were born, I did not consider their crying—at least not as newborns—as necessary evidence of an inherited proclivity to sin. Nor did I consider them totally depraved; instead, I thought of them as developing from less maturity to greater maturity. Thus, their mother and I worked continuously to help them learn things and make wise decisions. We cared about providing creative learning experiences and using discretion in terms of friends with whom they spent time, where they went to school, and where they went to church. In other words, we approached parenting as if our thoughts, words, and actions made a long-term difference in preparing our children for adulthood. My wife and

I read books, went to seminars, had conversations with friends, and prayed to God in order to become better parents, with the hope of our children becoming better people—people of Christian faith as well as character.

I do not know how one can approach parenting without the assumption that words and actions make a difference, that people can be better or worse parents, and that children can become better or worse people as they grow up. To be sure, I am not a perfect parent, and my children are not perfect. Of course, in addition to parents, there is a myriad of factors that influence the nurture of children: biology, culture, class, race, ethnicity, gender, language, and so on. But my approach to parenting was that both my children and I had freedom to make choices, and I wanted to raise my children in ways that would help them maximize future decision making to be knowledgeable, wise, and faithful.

It seems to me that human freedom, or what some call free will, is obvious in our day-to-day lives. Although our freedom may not be absolute because of limiting factors—spiritual as well as physical—that affect our lives, a measure of genuine free will exists. To think that our choices are determined (and are not free, ultimately speaking) requires powerful argumentation psychologically, philosophically, or theologically.

Surprisingly, quite a few people claim that their lives and decisions are determined and that they live more as observers than as participants in life. This deterministic view, whether it is biologically, psychologically, or theologically driven, has significant moral implications for society as well as for individuals. Theologically, Calvin's theology advocated the belief that people are powerfully influenced by God and God's will for their lives, and that sin also powerfully influences them, so much so that people today are unconditionally dependent upon God. Wesley also thought that God and sin powerfully influence people, but he did not think that people's freedom was as decimated, because of God's enabling grace. How Christians think about these matters strongly influences how they live day to day, how responsible they are for their decisions, and how they plan for the future. So it is important to talk about the differences between Wesley and Calvin, especially with regard to their understanding of humanity and of the nature and extent of human freedom.

Image of God and Sin

Both Wesley and Calvin believed that people are created in the image of God (Genesis 1:26-27). Calvin said, "For although God's glory shines forth

30

in the outer man, yet there is no doubt that the proper seat of his image is in the soul...provided it be regarded as a settled principle that the image of God, which is seen or glows in these outward marks, is spiritual."[1] Similarly, Wesley said:

> So God created man in his own image....Not barely in his *natural image,* a picture of his own immortality, a spiritual being endued with understanding, freedom of will, and various affections; nor merely in his *political image,* the governor of this lower world, having "dominion over the fishes of the sea, and over all the fowl of the air, and over the cattle, and over all the earth"; but chiefly in his *moral image,* which, according to the Apostle, is "righteousness and true holiness."[2]

Wesley and Calvin believed that God created humanity in a privileged way that reflected the image and likeness of God, all of which was part of God's good creation.

Among the various ways that people reflect the image of God is in their free will. However, human freedom can be a liability as well as a benefit. Having freedom makes one susceptible to wrong choices; unwise choices; evil choices. Both Wesley and Calvin believed that people had fallen from their privileged status, endowed through creation, and had sinned against God. If this was not bad enough, all of humanity has inherited the effects, which Wesley and Calvin described as "original sin." Calvin said, "Original sin, therefore, seems to be a hereditary depravity and corruption of our nature, diffused into all parts of the soul, which first makes us liable to God's wrath, then also brings forth in us those works which Scripture calls 'works of the flesh' [Gal. 5:19]."[3] For Calvin, depravity was more extensive than intensive; sin extends to all dimensions of life. Likewise, Wesley thought that the original sin of our ancestors left us with an image of God that is corrupt and thus in need of redemption. According to Wesley, the occurrence of sin corrupted people's life, knowledge, will, liberty, and happiness.[4]

Calvin thought that humanity had become irrevocably corrupted or depraved by the effects of original sin. He and Wesley spoke of human nature in two ways: on the one hand, they talked about human nature prior to the sinful fall of humanity; on the other hand, they talked about human nature after the fall of humanity—a nature branded by sin. Thus, it is important to know the particular context in which either man spoke about human nature.

To begin with, Wesley and Calvin disagreed about the explanation for people's original sin—that is, for their fall from created goodness. Calvin said that people are responsible: "Accordingly, man falls according as God's providence ordains, but he falls by his own fault."[5] So people are responsible for sin, but it occurs within the context of God's providence. But is not God's providence sovereign, all-encompassing, and meticulously decreed for every person, group, and nation? Calvin thought that the Bible clearly states that people are responsible for sin; yet, he equally thought that the Bible clearly states that God decreed (or predestined) what happens. Although these propositions seem contradictory, Calvin argued that they must be held together as part of God's "hidden" or secret plan, to which people are not privy. We must accept God's providence (and people's culpability for sin) without question, since all things occur for God's glory. Calvin said:

> Now we need bear only this in mind: man was far different at the first creation from his whole posterity, who, deriving their origin from him in his corrupted state, have contracted from him a hereditary taint. . . . But the reason he did not sustain man by the virtue of perseverance lies hidden in his plan; sobriety is for us the part of wisdom. Man, indeed, received the ability provided he exercised the will; but he did not have the will to use his ability, for this exercising of the will would have been followed by perseverance. Yet he is not excusable, for he received so much that he voluntarily brought about his own destruction; indeed, no necessity was imposed upon God of giving man other than a mediocre and even transitory will, that from man's Fall he might gather occasion for his own glory.[6]

When it comes to speaking about sin, Calvin affirmed that the responsibility lies with people, rather than God. Sin is always the fault of people, according to Calvin, on account of teachings of the Bible about sin. Although people's culpability for sin may seem incongruous to logic, given the sovereignty of God's decrees, Christians must humbly accept their guilt as part of God's eternal, albeit hidden, plan for humanity.

The question about who carries the ultimate responsibility for sin —people or God—was a question that arose immediately during the life of Calvin. Many in Geneva questioned the obvious implications of Calvin's view of divine providence and predestination. Most notably was Jérôme-Hermès Bolsec, who in 1551 criticized the theology of Calvin and accused him of making God the author of sin. As a result of his attack on what he considered the absurdities of Calvin's Reformed theology, Bolsec was banished from Geneva. So questions about the implications of Calvin's view of divine providence and predestination are not new, but such ideas were expelled from his presence as well as that of Geneva.

Similar to Bolsec, Arminius, and other critics of Calvin, Wesley did not believe that God's sovereignty, power, and glory precluded God's voluntary self-restriction of divine control over people, subsequent to the sinful fall of humanity. He thought that the Bible teaches a different view of God and the works of God. According to Wesley, God created people in the image of God and that God permitted them—by grace—to have and exercise genuine freedom of will, both prior to and after the fall. To be sure, mystery remains with regard to all the workings of God in relationship with people. But Wesley thought that Calvin could not avoid making God ultimately responsible for sin, since the latter argued so insistently for how God is the "determinative principle" of all that occurs.[7] Wesley disagreed both with Calvin's interpretation of the Bible and theological logic. It was not necessary, according to Wesley, to project upon the Bible a hidden will of God that affirms that God controls all events while at the same time affirms that people are responsible for sin. Both the Bible and church history provide theological explanations for how Christians may affirm both the sovereignty of God and people's responsibility.

No matter how much Calvin and his followers affirmed that God controls all events while not being held responsible for sin, Wesley disagreed. Wesley agreed that people are sinful and cannot save themselves, but Wesley disagreed with Calvin regarding why people are responsible for sin. By grace, God both permits and enables people to have a measure—albeit genuine measure—of responsibility. Again, by grace, they may decide to respond to the promptings of the Holy Spirit in their lives and accept God's gift of salvation; they may also decide to resist God's Spirit. Thus, people's culpability for sin is conditioned upon their decisions, rather than upon decisions God irresistibly predetermined before the foundation of the world.

Predestination and Sin

Both Wesley and Calvin believed in predestination; the Bible teaches about it. Predestination is often thought of in terms of God's determination of who is saved, but it is also used to describe God's determination of other circumstances as well. As such, predestination is related to the overall care of God for the world and people, which is known as "providence." Providence has to do with what God decrees for the world and people. Some—if not all—of God's decrees occurred before creation, before the "foundation of the world" (Ephesians 1:4). From a human perspective, such decrees seem predetermined—that is, determined previous to our experience and knowledge of God's providence here and now.

Wesley and Calvin had different views about the nature and extent of God's providential decrees. Calvin argued that God's providence touches upon everything that happens. He said, "From this we declare that not only heaven and earth and the inanimate creatures, but also the plans and intentions of men, are so governed by his providence that they are borne by it straight to their appointed end."[8] Sometimes Calvin's views are referred to as "meticulous providence," since God is thought meticulously to decree all that occurs, whether it has to do with the events of nature or the decisions of people. So much is this the case that, as previously noted, Calvin thought that God predestines those who will be saved and those who will be damned. He said: "We call predestination God's eternal decree, by which he compacted with himself what he willed to become of each man. For all are not created in equal condition; rather, eternal life is foreordained for some, eternal damnation for others. Therefore, as any man has been created to one or the other of these ends, we speak of him as predestined to life or to death."[9] Calvin, of course, did not think that this affirmation totally precluded human responsibility, since God wills that people act freely. In other words, God wills that people want to act the way they are foreordained to act. For Calvin, people possess what some Calvinists have called "compatibilist freedom," since people's free will choices are compatible with God's will. In fact, Calvin would say that people are only free when their thoughts, words, and actions conform to God's will—that is, to God's decrees. This understanding represents a logically consistent understanding, according to Calvin, and thus explains how people can be considered responsible for their actions prior to and after the fall. In this life, it is people who choose, not God. Calvin rejected alternative views of freedom that he deemed naturalistic, voluntaristic, or indeterminate. Such views of human freedom verged on Pelagianism—that is, belief that people naturally exercise free will without reference to God's sovereign governance of the world.

Wesley certainly did not believe in a naturalistic (or atheistic) understanding of human freedom. As already mentioned, he opposed the beliefs of Pelagianism, which emphasize works righteousness with regard to salvation. In The Articles of Religion, Wesley affirmed of Methodism, "Original sin standeth not in the following of Adam (as the Pelagians do vainly talk)."[10] Because of sin, people have no innate human ability to earn or merit their salvation. In this regard, Wesley agreed with the Reformed belief that the sin nature is inherited. Unlike Pelagianism, Wesley did not think that people naturally have the wherewithal to live righteously and thus merit salvation.

Even so, Wesley thought that Calvin—like Augustine—had too narrowly conceived of the theological options for understanding divine predestination and human freedom. Basically speaking, they considered only two options: Augustine and Pelagius (or Augustinianism and Pelagianism). When people think of issues in only two ways, it precludes the complexity of how they are discussed in the Bible as well as how they have been discussed in church history. Instead Wesley argued that Augustine overreacted to Pelagius (and other variations of Pelagianism, known as Semi-Pelagianism), emphasizing not only a deterministically oriented predestinarianism but also the kind of absolute predestinarianism Calvin suggested. In a dialogical discussion that Wesley created between "a predestinarian and his friend," Wesley spoke about the history of predestinarianism. He said:

> Augustine speaks sometimes for it and sometimes against it. But all antiquity for the four first centuries is against you [i.e., the predestinarianism], as is the whole Eastern Church to this day; and the Church of England, both in her Catechism, Articles, and Homilies. And so are divers of our most holy Martyrs, Bishop Hooper and Bishop Latimer in particular.[11]

Wesley considered his Semi-Augustinian viewpoint to be consistent with the longest standing tradition of Christianity, going back to the Bible and the ancient patristic authors. His theological heritage, with regard to issues of divine predestination and human freedom, did not flow from Augustine or the magisterial Protestant reformers like Luther and Calvin who conceived of the human will as being in utter bondage. Likewise, in contradistinction to the Reformed theology of Jonathan Edwards, who was a contemporary of his in the American colonies, Wesley said:

> I cannot possibly allow the consequences, upon Mr. Edwards's supposition....For their will, on your supposition, is irresistibly impelled; so that they cannot help will thus or thus. If so, they are no more blamable for that will, than for the actions which follow it. There is no blame if they are under necessity of willing. There can be no moral good or evil, unless they have liberty as well as will.[12]

Instead Wesley followed the historic theological views of Roman Catholicism, Orthodox churches, and Anglicanism, which viewed human freedom as a gracious gift of God available prior to the fall, and that continued to be available—albeit in diminished form—after the fall. By means of the prevenient (also known as preceding, prevening, or preventing) work of grace, God permits a measure of freedom, through the Holy Spirit, which is sufficient for people to act responsibly.

Augustine had talked about prevenient grace, but he did not think that such grace could be resisted. In contrast, most Christians in the ancient church thought that prevenient grace enabled a measure of genuine freedom on the part of individuals to decide, for example, with regard to God's offer of the gift of salvation. But such grace did not ensure someone's decision, since God also permits people—by divine grace—to sin. Consequently, people past and present are guilty of their sin because of their own decisions—decisions not predetermined irresistibly by God but determined by people to resist God. As such, people are without excuse for their sin.

35

Double Predestination

The election to eternal life and the reprobation to eternal damnation are sometimes referred to as "double predestination," which Wesley described as the view of absolute predestination. Calvin did not use either term, but the concept of double predestination is implied throughout his theology. For example, Calvin wrote, "God is said to have ordained from eternity those whom he wills to embrace in love and those upon whom he wills to vent his wrath."[13] Clearly Calvin maintained that God elects some, and God reprobates others. This dual election and reprobation is what later Calvinists called "double predestination," which they embraced in description of their Reformed theology. Calvin drew upon biblical passages such as Romans 9–11 in order to make his case for how God unconditionally predestined the eternal state of everyone, how all is determined for the glory of God, and how Christians ought not to question God's decrees.

God did not predetermine the eternal state of people based upon God's eternal knowledge (or foreknowledge) that conditions or influences God's decrees. On the contrary, God's decrees are unconditioned, uninfluenced by any thoughts, words, or deeds on the part of people. God's election and reprobation are entirely because of the will of God, and Christians in particular ought to beware of trying to fathom the decrees of God. Calvin said, "He who here seeks a deeper cause than God's secret and inscrutable plan will torment himself to no purpose."[14]

Calvin followed the theological tradition of both Augustine and Luther, who believed that God elected some to be saved. However, neither Augustine nor Luther went as far as Calvin in saying that God elected some to be damned. In this regard, the theological views of Augustine and Luther are sometimes called "single predestination," arguing that the Bible clearly states that some are elected for eternal life, while others are passed over. This view of being passed over is also known as "preterition"—that is, God's neglect of the damned, rather than God's direct damning of them. However, Calvin thought that affirmation of the sovereignty of God demanded that God be understood as directly decreeing the eternal states of everyone. Although followers of Calvin debate the precise order of God's decrees (e.g., supralapsarianism, vis-à-vis, infralapsarianism), God's predestination is absolute and not conditioned upon any human response. To Calvin, the mystery of electing some to be saved and others to be damned was no less dreadful than the mystery of why God elects some and neglects others. Thus, Christians ought to be bold in their claims about the decrees of God, rather than shy away from the logic of theological implications just because such divine decrees make people feel uncomfortable.

36

Wesley did not agree with the Reformed theological formulations of either single or double predestination. With regard to single predestination, he thought that Christians such as Augustine and Luther could not biblically or logically argue for it. Wesley said:

> You still believe that in consequence of an unchangeable, irresistible decree of God the greater part of mankind abide in death, without any possibility of redemption: inasmuch as none can save them but God; and he will not save them. You believe he hath absolutely decreed not to save them; and what is this but decreeing to damn them? It is, in effect, neither more nor less; it comes to the same thing. For if you are dead, and altogether unable to make yourself alive; then if God hath absolutely decreed your everlasting death—you are absolutely consigned to damnation. So then, though you use softer words than some [e.g., preterition or single predestination], you mean the selfsame thing.[15]

With regard to the double predestinarian implications of Calvin's theology, Wesley's words were more to the point. He rejected all theological variations of Calvinism, regardless of the theological language used: "'election,' 'preterition,' 'predestination' or 'reprobation'—it comes in the end to the same thing."[16]

From Wesley's perspective, Calvin diminished the sovereignty of God as well as God's other attributes of love, holiness, righteousness, justice, and goodness. Instead, Wesley thought that if God is unchangeable, then God's unchangeable loving and good character toward those who accept the gift of eternal life are included. God only judges those who choose to remain in sin. According to Wesley, "God is unchangeable with regard to his decrees. But what decrees? The same that he has commanded to be preached to every creature: 'He that believeth shall be saved; he that believeth not shall be damned.'"[17]

God's election is not based upon eternal decrees without conditions, but upon the foreknowledge of God. According to Wesley, God is one "to whom all things are present at once, who sees all eternity at one view," and God knows who will be convinced of grace as the "elect from the foundation of the world."[18] To people, such knowledge is considered foreknowledge, since it seems to occur before their lives. Indeed, people are limited to the finite duration of time, which they experience as past, present, and future. However, God's knowledge is eternal and not limited in the same way as people's experience of time.

Wesley's understanding of election had more to do with the general will of God for all people, rather than the specific will of God, which God effectually—that is, irresistibly—works in the lives of individuals. From our finite human perspective, it is difficult to understand the transcendent attributes of God's eternity, omnipresence, and omniscience. Wesley believed that God could be said to know the future, which is how people conceive of God's eternal knowledge. But they cannot fully comprehend it, since they are limited by space and time, consisting of a past, present, and future. However, God is not limited in the same way and knows all things as though they are present.

Foreknowledge is not causative knowledge. God knows our future because God knows such events from eternity. In a sense, those events inform God's knowledge, and before they occurred in our lives, God chose to interact with people in order to save them and bless their lives. Such knowledge to us, of course, is not fully understandable; it remains a mystery. And to a certain extent, all our theological affirmations about God, God's attributes, and God's governance ultimately transcend our finite human knowledge. Yet, because of the teachings of the Bible, we can speak meaningfully and plausibly about such matters because God has chosen to make them known. From Wesley's perspective, the Bible talks far more about how human freedom is compatible with divine sovereignty, rather than eliminated by it. Thus, biblical teaching about God's foreknowledge provides an explanation of how Christians may affirm both divine predestination and human freedom, without appealing to Calvin's explanation, which is as horrible as it is hidden.

Despite limitations in our knowledge of the person and work of God's Holy Spirit, Wesley was convinced that God did not exclude human freedom but graciously enabled it. People are not saved or damned exclusively by God's decrees, but by cooperation between them, enabled by divine grace. To think otherwise, according to Wesley, precluded belief in a God who is loving and just: "Justice can have no place in rewarding or punishing mere machines."[19] Elsewhere Wesley said: "How can the Judge of all the earth consign them [i.e., the reprobate] to everlasting fire, for what was in effect his own act and deed?"[20]

Free Will = Free Grace

Perhaps it is improper to speak of free will in relationship to Wesley's theology because he preferred to speak of it as "free grace." In his sermon "Free Grace," Wesley said: "How freely does God love the world!... The grace or love of God, whence cometh our salvation, is free in all, and free for all.... It does not depend on any power or merit in man.... They are not the cause, but the effects of it. Whatsoever good is in man, or is done by man, God is the author and doer of it."[21] Theologically speaking, people's ability to choose is not natural; God originally endowed it, and it continues to be grace enabled.

God graciously initiates human freedom, sustains it, and completes it without transgressing people's genuine ability to accept or reject God's gracious relations with them. Thus, free grace should remain more prominent in our theological discussion than free will, since it is God who brings the spiritual increase.

Free grace (or human freedom) can refer to several dimensions of people's lives. Let me begin with salvation: To what degree are people involved in their salvation? Despite the effects of sin, Wesley believed that people still have sufficient freedom to choose to have faith and repent of their sins, by God's grace, and thus receive the divine gift of salvation. In this regard, he does not disagree in the least with the Reformation principle of justification by grace through faith. Wesley said:

> [Salvation] is free in all to whom it is given. It does not depend on any power or merit in man; no, not in any degree, neither in whole, nor in part. It does not in any wise depend either on the good works or righteousness of the receiver; not on anything he has done, or anything he is. It does not depend on his endeavors. It does not depend on his good tempers, or good desires, or good purposes and intentions; for all these flow from the free grace of God.[22]

People choose to receive God's free gift of salvation because God provides the gracious wherewithal to do so. Wesley said, "How is it more for the glory of God to save man irresistibly, than to save him as a free agent, by such grace as he may either concur with or resist?"[23] From his perspective, the glory of God shone greater through God's thoroughly loving moral character, rather than through sheer power. It is a greater good that love may occur within the context of reciprocity—of giving and receiving love—rather than in a one-sided way that trivializes people's relationship with God.

God's election of people for salvation occurs because God foreknows those who will freely receive grace and have faith for salvation. As the Apostle Paul said, "For those whom he foreknew he also predestined to be conformed to the image of his Son, in order that he might be the firstborn within a large family" (Romans 8:29). Wesley believed in divine election, but it had more to do with a general election than a particular (or meticulous) election. The former makes grace available to all, whereas the latter makes saving grace available only to the few who are elect.

Throughout church history, the majority of Christians did not consider it an offense to the glory and majesty of God to believe that God intentionally limited divine power over people in order for them to exercise genuine human freedom, despite the risk of sin and evil. In fact, divine self-limitation should be viewed as a more holistic expression of sovereignty, because a greater good occurs than if people are always controlled, as in a divine determinism. To be sure, free will is not easily identifiable or sustainable, especially in a world so cognizant of the powerful factors than constrain our decision making: biology, relationships, culture, economics, politics, and so on. But Wesley thought that the Bible as well as the ancient church and experience confirmed the genuineness of our choice to do one thing rather than another, even if it included doing that which God does not want us to do.

Obviously, Calvin did not speak of his theology in terms of determinism. After all, is not determinism a philosophical term that is not biblical, not Calvin's own words, and not actually more of an intrusion of culture upon Christian theology? Well, to begin with, Christians highly value many words and phrases that are not explicitly found in the Bible; for example, Trinity, Incarnation, virgin birth, salvation by faith alone, and—for that matter—Bible. They are affirmations that developed in church history, though they are considered commensurate with the Bible.

Second, although theological words may not be found explicitly in the Bible, they may rightly characterize the beliefs, values, and practices of Christians. Especially in comparing and contrasting men such as Wesley and Calvin, philosophical and extrabiblical terms can be useful in analyzing and evaluating theological concepts. Do such usages run the risk of projecting nonbiblical concepts onto the Bible? Of course, such a risk exists. However, because the New Testament was itself written in Greek, using Greek words and concepts, was there a risk of projecting Greek culture onto the first-century writings of the apostles? (To complicate matters, the New Testament also includes Hebrew, Aramaic, and Latin words, and possibly their cultural influence.) Again, there are risks involved. But most Christians throughout church history have believed that such influences were not destructive of God's revelation from being communicated. Likewise, use of terms such as determinism in analyzing and evaluating Calvin's systematic theology is not categorically destructive in understanding him.

Monergism and Synergism

To be sure, Calvin formulated his theology in determinist-oriented ways that greatly affirm God's freedom, but not the freedom of people. Calvin said: "[W]e ought undoubtedly to hold that whatever changes are discerned in the world are produced from the secret stirring of God's hand. But what God has determined must necessarily so take place, even though it is neither unconditionally, nor of its own peculiar nature, necessary."[24] Sometimes Calvin's emphasis on the determinative will of God is described as "monergism" (Greek, "one" + "work"). It means that one divine power is at work, which created all that exists and governs all that occurs. Followers of Calvin often embraced monergism as a way to explain their theological affirmations about how neither life nor salvation occurs outside of God's superintendence. To believe otherwise, they argue, is to put glory in people, rather than God, and affirm works righteousness, rather than salvation by grace through faith.

Wesley disagreed. He affirmed salvation by grace through faith, and that a more dynamic understanding is required by the Bible as well as by the majority of church tradition, critical thinking, and relevant experience that confirms people's responsibility in decision making. Sometimes Wesley's emphasis on the dynamic relationship people have with God is described as "synergism" (Greek, "together" + "work"). It means that divine power is at work in cooperation with power that God graciously provides to people. *Synergism* was not a word Wesley used, though the reality of synergistic reasoning was not new to him. On the contrary, most Christian writings in the ancient church as well as today resemble synergism far more than monergism.

When I teach about monergism and synergism, I tell students that each view—from a logical perspective—does not answer every question that we can imagine. Mystery persists with each view since, ultimately speaking, we do not comprehend fully God, who is transcendent and whose works surpass our understanding. Each theological point of view mentioned above has certain benefits and liabilities, logically speaking, and sometimes we can do little more than decide which mysteries we are willing to live with and which ones we are not. For example, how much of life is determined, and how much of it is because of people's decisions or because of circumstances beyond their control? How much of salvation is determined, and how much is because of people or circumstances?

Despite uncertainty, we can make coherent determinations with regard to what the Bible says in relationship to our salvation and life circumstances. The benefits of Calvin's theology is that he strongly affirms the sovereignty of God; if his beliefs challenge our understanding of the freedom of humanity and the origin of sin, then we must humbly accept them. The benefits of Wesley's theology is that he strongly affirms human freedom, not believing that it excludes the sovereignty of God; if his beliefs cannot easily discern the degree to which God is responsible and people are responsible for salvation and life decisions, then we must humbly accept them.

Because Calvin thought of salvation in terms of causation, he wanted to affirm that it is God who causes it rather than people. Calvin said:

> Moreover, although our mind cannot apprehend God without rendering some honor to him, it will not suffice simply to hold that there is One whom all ought to honor and adore, unless we are also persuaded that he is the fountain of every good, and that we must seek nothing elsewhere than in him. This I take to mean that... no drop will be found either of wisdom and light, or of righteousness or power or rectitude, or of genuine truth, which does not flow from him, and of which he is not the cause.

Wesley, however, thought of salvation more relationally. God does not merely want to save people juridically from their sinful condition—to provide the sufficient cause for their justification. God wants reconciliation with people so that there may be renewed fellowship, characterized by love as well as by other fruit of the Spirit: "joy, peace, patience, kindness, generosity, faithfulness, gentleness, and self-control" (Galatians 5:22-23).

The freedom to accept God's salvation, of course, does not end with conversion. Christians are called to act freely, by the grace of God, to grow in their love and relationship with God for the remainder of life. They act synergistically in relationship with the Holy Spirit, who in turns sanctifies them into greater Christlikeness by renewing the pristine image of God in which they were originally created.

Let me end with a quotation that typifies Wesley's emphasis on love—on the love God has for people, and on the love people are to have, in turn, in relationship with God. He said:

> It were well you should be thoroughly sensible of this, "The heaven of heavens is love." There is nothing higher in religion; there is, in effect, nothing else; if you look for anything more than love, you are looking wide of the mark, you are getting out of the royal way, and when you are asking others, "Have you received this or that blessing?" if you mean anything but more love, you mean wrong; you are leading them out of the way, and putting them upon a false scent. Settle it then in your heart, that from the moment God has saved you from all sin, you are to aim at nothing more, but more of that love described in the thirteenth of the Corinthians. You can go no higher than this, till you are carried into Abraham's bosom.[25]

Final Thoughts

Both Wesley and Calvin believed in the sinfulness of humanity, of people's fallenness and alienation from God, and of their impossible situation relative to eternal life. But God did not leave people without hope of salvation. Wesley and Calvin celebrated how God provided salvation through the life, death, and resurrection of Jesus Christ. By grace, Christians are saved through faith; it is a gift that they do not merit or for which they work.

Calvin believed that God unilaterally acted on behalf of human beings, saving them from a totally depraved state of sin. Wesley believed that God initiated salvation, enables it by grace, and completes the salvation of people. According to Wesley, God does not unilaterally save people. God expects people to cooperate in salvation, since it involves a genuine, uncoerced choice to become reconciled with God. The choice is not a natural ability; God makes it possible by graciously permitting people to choose to accept salvation, to have a personal relationship with God, and to love freely. Such freedom continues throughout the lives of Christians, always by God's grace, giving them hope of growing into greater Christlikeness and of expressing love to God and others, individually and socially.

Discussion Questions

1. What does it mean for you to be created in the image of God?

2. What are the effects of sin in your life? How totally depraved do you consider yourself and others to be?

3. How do you understand God's salvation for humanity?

4. Do you think that God predestines only those who are to be saved? All those who are to be saved as well as those who are to be damned? Only those who God foreknows will believe?

5. How free do you think people are? For salvation? For day-to-day life?

6. To what degree do you think of salvation as forgiveness of sins, and to what degree to you think of salvation as reconciliation with God? Are they contradictory views? Complementary views?

Chapter 4

GRACE: MORE PREVENIENT THAN IRRESISTIBLE

According to the grace of God given to me, like a skilled master builder I laid a foundation, and someone else is building on it. Each builder must choose with care how to build on it. (1 Corinthians 3:10)

One of the best-known hymns is entitled "Amazing Grace," written by John Newton. The words are memorable; they have to do with how God helps people when they cannot help themselves. In particular, the words have to do with salvation and how God redeems people who are lost to sin, fear, and the dangers of life. Consider the words of the hymn, which Newton published in 1779, along with his collaborator William Cowper, in the *Olney Hymns*:

> Amazing grace! (how sweet the sound)
> That sav'd a wretch like me!
> I once was lost, but now am found,
> Was blind, but now I see.

> Thro' many dangers, toils, and snares,
> I have already come;
> 'Tis grace hath brought me safe thus far,
> And grace will lead me home.

> The Lord has promis'd good to me,
> His word my hope secures;
> He will my shield and portion be
> As long as life endures.

Yes, when this flesh and heart shall fail,
And mortal life shall cease;
I shall possess, within the veil,
A life of joy and peace.

The earth shall soon dissolve like snow,
The sun forbear to shine;
But God, who call'd me here below,
Will be forever mine.

The theme that threads throughout the hymn is grace—God's grace. Newton had lived a tumultuous life, and he was familiar with how desperate life can be. He had served in the British navy and eventually became the captain of a slave-trading ship, which captured men, women, and children in Africa and sold them as slaves in the Americas. While on a voyage at sea, Newton experienced conversion in a way that eventually led him to forsake the slave trade and pursue ministry. He actually knew John Wesley, who encouraged him to become ordained in the Church of England. After becoming the curate in Olney, Newton became friends with Cowper, and the two men were successful in promoting evangelically oriented Christianity as well as hymnody.

The hymn "Amazing Grace" became popular in the United States during the Second Great Awakening, when revivals spread throughout the country in the nineteenth century. Its words were also popular among abolitionists, as recorded in the novel *Uncle Tom's Cabin,* written by Harriet Beecher Stowe. In the novel, the slave named Tom sang "Amazing Grace" during times of despair. Stowe included words not written by Newton but that were part of African American oral tradition:

When we've been there ten thousand years,
Bright shining as the sun,
We've no less days to sing God's praise,
Than when we first begun.

These words are as compelling today as they were in the past, which is why the hymn of "Amazing Grace" continues to be so popular.

The theme of grace was prominent in the writings of both Wesley and Calvin. They considered God's grace essential to their beliefs, values, and practices. Yet Wesley and Calvin had different views of the way that God graciously works in and through the lives of people. In order to understand them, it is critical to investigate how each man viewed God's amazing grace.

What Is Grace?

Grace has variously been defined as divine "favor," "kindness," or "gratitude" for God's blessings; it has also been thought of as including divine "empowerment." The etymology of the word comes from Greek, *charis,* and Latin, *gratia.* Certainly grace became a prominent belief in the Protestant Reformation because of the emphasis upon *sola gratia* (Latin, "grace alone") with regard to salvation and the forgiveness of sin. People cannot spiritually redeem themselves by their own work, effort, or merit. According to the Apostle Paul, salvation is a gift and not a matter of human achievement. He said, "For by grace you have been saved through faith, and this is not your own doing; it is the gift of God—not the result of works, so that no one may boast" (Ephesians 2:8-9).

Calvin as well as Luther considered God's grace the only active power involved in people's salvation. Because of sin and the total depravity of people, God alone must work to elect some to salvation. People are expected to respond in faith, which is why another Protestant affirmation was *sola fide* (Latin, "faith alone"). But even people's faith was not thought to be a part of the work or merit of salvation. There was no synergistic or cooperative dynamic thought to exist between God and people, since faith is a result of divine grace rather than any human involvement. Grace works effectually in the lives of people; God brings to effect salvation in people, which God decreed before the foundation of the world.

Wesley also believed in salvation by grace through faith, alluding to Ephesians 2:8-9. God saves people; people do not merit their salvation and forgiveness of sin. Yet Wesley did not think that grace works effectually—that is, that grace is always efficacious and accomplishes the will of God without decisive response on the part of people. He thought that grace comes from God to people beforehand by what is known as "prevenient grace"—grace that "comes before." Such grace initiates, sustains, and completes people's ability to respond to God's grace, so people cannot be thought of as having worked for or merited their salvation. But people should be thought of as having chosen to accept or receive the offer of salvation that God makes to them through the atonement of Jesus Christ. These beliefs about prevenient grace were not new to Wesley; Christians in the Anglo-Catholic tradition had believed them for centuries. Let us look further at the difference between the ways that Wesley and Calvin believed and acted with regard to God's grace.

Effectual Grace

Calvin believed that God works effectually (effectively, or efficaciously) in the lives of people because of God's sovereign rule. The grace of God cannot be resisted because people do not possess the ability to add or subtract from their spiritual well-being. Only God saves people, and it is God who decrees their destiny, temporally and eternally. When it comes to salvation, people's faith is "merely passive." Calvin said:

> Therefore, we must come to this remedy: that believers should be convinced that their only ground of hope for the inheritance of a Heavenly Kingdom lies in the fact that, being engrafted in the body of Christ, they are freely accounted righteous. For, as regards justification, faith is something merely passive, bringing nothing of ours to the recovering of God's favor but receiving from Christ that which we lack.[1]

Even people's obedient good works, subsequent to conversion, are the result of divine grace and not of human initiation. In this regard, Calvin considered himself to be consistent with both the Bible and Augustine when he said, "Grace alone brings about every good work."[2]

Calvin disagreed with Roman Catholics, who argue that people are to "co-operate with the assisting grace of God, because it is our right either to render it ineffectual by spurning the first grace, or to confirm it by obediently following it."[3] Whether it is called "assisting grace" or "accepting grace," Calvin did not think that people should be thought of as having any genuine power toward their spiritual and eternal lives. Such matters are the work of God and not of people.

Later followers of Calvin talked about God's effectual grace as being "irresistible." Calvin did not use the language of irresistibility, but he did talk about the effectual nature of divine grace and how God will effect (carry out, or accomplish) God's plans for people and the world. When the Bible suggests that God tries or tests people, Calvin argued that such is not technically the case, since it would imply that people have some natural or spiritual ability to assist or resist divine grace. Instead, he said that such instances serve to humble people and to remind them of their "nothingness." Calvin says, "He [i.e., God] does both to make us more humble. . . . [W]e falsely gather that we have some power of free will for him to observe and test. For he does it for no other purpose than to compel us to recognize our own nothingness."[4]

Prevenient Grace

Wesley emphasized the prevenient role of divine grace in the lives of people—the grace that comes before from God in advance of human response. The concept of prevenient grace was commonplace within the Church of England in which Wesley was raised. Prevenient grace, also known as "preventing grace" or "prevening grace," refers to God's universal work in the

47

lives of people to draw them to God. Nowadays the word *preventing* suggests obstruction or stopping, but in Wesley's day the word meant preparing or making possible. God's grace makes it possible for people to respond to divine initiation with regard to salvation as well as other dimensions of Christian living. In relationship to the Bible, the mechanics or process of how this works may remain a mystery, but the reality of human freedom and responsibility is undeniable in the Bible as well as in life. People need to respond for their salvation, just as they need to respond if they are considered culpable of sin. Prevenient grace makes it possible for people to respond or not respond to the gift of salvation and to other blessings (and conditions) God gives to people. Specifically, with regard to salvation, Wesley said that prevenient grace elicits "the first wish to please God, the first dawn of light concerning his will, and the first slight transient conviction of having sinned against him."[5]

In contrast, Calvin affirmed salvation by grace alone and through faith alone, by which he meant that salvation occurs through the immediate action of divine omnipotence, rather than through the mediate action of people. There are no means of grace by which cooperation with convincing and justifying grace occurs—that is, there are no means or conditions of salvation for people. God's omnipotence—God's power and will—is absolute. Thus, divine grace is irresistible; people can neither resist nor cooperate efficaciously with it. Likewise, God's election is unconditional; there are no conditions or prerequisites on the part of people for their salvation.

Wesley did not think of the synergistically oriented relationship between God and people to be a natural work on the part of people that somehow merited salvation, as if people were responsible for their eternal life, rather than God. This is why Wesley talked about free grace (rather than free will) as a more accurate description of people's involvement in salvation and the Christian life, since people still require the empowering work of God's grace. Calvin would have disagreed with Wesley, of course, because Calvin thought that any conditionality afforded to people, even by grace, detracted from God's sovereignty, power, and majesty. However, according to Wesley, people are thought to have a genuine—not irresistible—role in becoming reconciled to God, who desires believers to love God freely as well as receive freely the gift of eternal life provided by Jesus' atonement. Through the ongoing, dynamic relationship people have with God's Holy Spirit, salvation and the Christian life should be thought of in more dynamic, relational ways, rather than static, irresistible ways that consider salvation a mere legal transaction and not as important as renewed fellowship with God.

In this regard, Wesley again considered himself to be in the longstanding tradition of Christianity, which could be traced back through the Protestant Reformation in England, Catholicism, ancient orthodoxy, and the Bible. Despite Calvin's popularity among Protestants and the appealing systematic nature of his theology, he was not within the historic mainstream of Christians on the topic of divine grace, especially with regard to the prevenient ways in which God interacts with people. To be sure, Calvin is essential for those who claim to be part of the Reformed tradition, and Calvin, as well as the Reformed tradition, has been extensively influential among Protestants. But not all Protestants are either Calvinist or Reformed; in fact, the majority of Protestants probably reflect more the Catholic, Orthodox, and Anglican views of grace as prevenient found in Wesley.

Part of the reason people do not know this—in addition to their general lack of historical perspective—is because they have inadequate terms for categorizing differences of theological opinion among Christians. Again, a common misconception arises when debate over God's role and people's role is thought to be between either Augustinianism or Pelagianism. Since ancient Christians considered Pelagianism a heresy, what alternative might one have other than to be Augustinian? (This woeful ignorance of theological categories is especially widespread among Protestants.) However, even Augustine talked about Semi-Pelagians, as already noted. But, the theological traditions upon which Wesley drew his ideas were neither Pelagian nor Semi-Pelagian. Instead they were more a variation of Augustinianism—what is best described as Semi-Augustinianism, since its adherents argue that God graciously initiates as well as sustains and completes people's salvation.

God is thought to limit voluntarily God's own power over people, which does not represent a genuine limitation in God's sovereignty, so that people may act responsibly and not irresistibly. By means of God's prevenient work of grace, which is universally available through the Holy Spirit in the lives of people, people may genuinely respond without God effectually determining their choices. When people do not respond, of course, then they are thought to be genuinely responsible for sin and evil that occurs. Sin and evil do not occur irresistibly, because of God's sovereignty and irresistible grace, but through people's active rebellion or passive indifference to God.

Again, Wesley's views were not unique or innovative. They represent the majority view of Christians throughout church history. Despite Augustine's theological prominence in church history, most of the ancient and medieval Christians rejected his absolute predestinarianism. Luther and Calvin revived Augustinian beliefs and values. But Anglicans did not agree, nor did Arminians. The majority of Christians around the world today—Catholics, Orthodox, Anglican, and the majority of Protestants—agree with Wesley in practice, if not also in theory. It is largely those in the Lutheran and Reformed traditions who promote Augustinian views of predestination. More and more, Christians accept the Semi-Augustinian view as best representative of the Bible and life experience.

Can God graciously act irresistibly in the lives of people and in the world? Of course, Wesley would say. After all, God is sovereign and can do whatever God wants. God can absolutely direct the lives of people and the course of history, if God chooses to do so. That is just the point. God does not choose to do so—at least not all the time. God graciously created the world and people with a measure of freedom. This was God's choice, and it was not a limitation upon God's power but an expression of God's love. God did not want to create robotlike people whose actions are irresistibly determined. Instead God wanted to create people with sufficient freedom to communicate with God and to love God, even though such provision may result in people rejecting God and the blessings involved with salvation. To be sure, there are mysteries involved with the theological logic of both Wesley and Calvin, which have become the topics of prolonged debates among Christians throughout church history. Wesley, however, believed that the evidence of the Bible as well as that of experience confirmed the prevenient—rather than irresistible—relationship God initiated with people by grace.

Two Stories

The grace of God affects the lives of people for more than their salvation. It affects all dimensions of their lives. Prevenient grace does not relate to conversion only; it relates to the whole of life, especially Christian life. As God works in our lives, we in turn—by God's grace—ought to work in accordance with God as attested in the Bible. Wesley said: "God worketh in you; therefore, you must work: You must be 'workers together with him,' (they are the very words of the Apostle,) otherwise he will cease working. . . . Go on, in virtue of the grace of God, preventing, accompanying, and following you, in 'the work of faith, in the patience of hope, and the labour of love.'"[6] Christians' work, effort, and accomplishments do not merit salvation, but they reflect the ongoing presence of divine grace through the Holy Spirit. Calvin, like Wesley, thought that believers ought to live obedient lives in accordance with the laws of God as attested in the Bible. But Calvin had a different motivation for why people are to act obediently, which will be the subject of discussion in the chapter on Christian spirituality.

The prevenience, vis-à-vis, irresistibility of grace, can be illustrated in the writings of Wesley and Calvin. Perhaps the contrast can best be clarified through two stories (or narratives) told by them, having to do with the degree to which God acts—graciously—in the lives of people. The stories have to do with more than salvation and more than the Christian life. They have to do with how God works—irresistibly or preveniently—in all dimensions of people's lives.

Calvin told the first story in order to talk about how God is ultimately in control of life events, regardless of whether good or bad things seem to happen. Again, because God is ultimately in control, no events can truly be thought to be bad or, at least, outside the eternal will of God. No events are fortuitous or happen unexpectedly, since God irresistibly ordains all things. Calvin said:

> Let us imagine, for example, a merchant who, entering a wood with a com-
> pany of faithful men, unwisely wanders away from his companions, and
> in his wandering comes upon a robber's den, falls among thieves, and is
> slain. His death was not only foreseen by God's eye, but also determined by
> his decree. For it is not said that he foresaw how long the life of each man
> would extend, but that he determined and fixed the bounds that men can-
> not pass [Job 14:5]. Yet as far as the capacity of our mind is concerned, all
> things therein seem fortuitous. What will a Christian think at this point?
> Just this: whatever happened in a death of this sort he will regard as fortu-
> itous by nature, as it is; yet he will not doubt that God's providence exer-
> cised authority over fortune in directing its end. The same reckoning applies
> to the contingency of future events.[7]

All occurs by the grace of God, regardless of whether—from a human perspective—events seem good or bad, promoting life or ending it. On the one
hand, Calvin argued that the good comes from God, and on the other hand,
the bad (including sin and evil) comes from people (Satan notwithstanding).
Although he consistently argued for the effectual nature of grace and the sovereign will of God in directing the events of life, it remains problematic as to
how sin and evil occur. Calvin seems to give God all the credit for the good
that occurs, while at the same time placing the culpability upon people and
absolving God from responsibility for pain, suffering, sin, or evil. To repeat,
it seems difficult to accept the logic that God should be glorified for all that
occurs, while at the same time censuring those whose lives God irresistibly
directs.

By contrast, Wesley told a story about calling people to convert—to believe and repent of their sin. He considered such calls to conversion to be
genuine; subsequently, by God's grace, people must decide for themselves
whether they respond or not. Their eternal lives as well as their temporal
lives depend upon it. Wesley told the following story in order to contrast his

beliefs with those of Calvin, and indeed challenged Calvinist ideas about the irresistibility of grace. Wesley said:

> Our blessed Lord does indisputably command and invite "all men every where to repent." He calleth all. He sends his ambassadors, in his name, to "preach the gospel to every creature." He himself "preached deliverance to the captives," without any hint of restriction or limitation. But now, in what manner do you [Calvinists] represent him, while he is employed in this work? You suppose him to be standing at the prison-doors, having the keys thereof in his hands, and to be continually inviting the prisoners to come forth, commanding them to accept of that invitation, urging every motive which can possibly induce them to comply with that command; adding the most precious promises, if they obey, the most dreadful threatenings, if they obey not; and all this time you suppose him to be unalterably determined in himself never to open the doors for them! Even while he is crying, "Come ye, come ye from that evil place: For why will ye die, O house of Israel!" "Why!" might one of them reply, "because we cannot help it. We cannot help ourselves; and thou wilt not help us."...Alas! My brethren, what kind of sincerity is this, which you ascribe to God our Saviour?[8]

Clearly, Wesley considered the beliefs of "Mr. Calvin" to be contrary not only to the teachings of the Bible but also to the justice and love of God.[9] By contrast, Calvin thought that his beliefs should encourage people because their salvation rests entirely outside of their responsibility. Indeed, Calvin considered it a great comfort that people not be held accountable for their eternal and spiritual well-being. They may rest assured in knowing that God is in complete control of all that occurs. But Wesley thought that people's responsibility in no way diminished divine sovereignty, assurance of salvation by grace through faith, or life in the Spirit of God. Indeed it represented a greater affirmation of God's sovereignty, love, justice, and other attributes of God because of the relational, responsible ways that God's Spirit graciously works in relationship with people.

Types of Grace

Wesley and Calvin talked about different types of grace. So in order to understand their beliefs and practices more fully, it is important to discuss the differences. For example, Calvin believed in a "general grace" that God gives to people.[10] Later Calvinists describe this grace as "common grace," though Calvin does not use the phrase. General grace refers to the divine enabling given to all people, which contributes to the diversity among people as well as constrains their sin and evil from leading to the destruction of one another.

In this sense, general grace represents undeserved benefits from God in the current lives of all people; its benefits are temporal. General grace does not lead people to salvation; God's "special grace," or effectual grace, is required for salvation, and God does not supply special grace to everyone. Calvin said: "Now, because some are born fools or stupid, that defect does not obscure the general grace of God.... For why is one person more excellent than another? Is it not to display in common nature God's special grace, which, in passing many by, declares itself bound to none?"[11] God does not give special, saving grace to everyone, but everyone benefits from God's general grace. Calvin thought that general grace reveals a trace of the image of God in people, which is why there exists so much individuality as well as variety among people with regard to their personalities, intellect, and accomplishments. He especially connected general grace with the third use of divine law, namely, its moral use as a guide to the elect as well as the reprobate for how they should live moral lives. Government, in particular, benefits from the laws of God, since such laws helped establish more just and orderly governance among people.[12] Indeed, God implants the law upon people—for example, as found in the Ten Commandments—through the work of general grace. So people benefit greatly from it both individually and collectively. Still, general grace is temporal and has no direct impact upon people's salvation.

Calvin's belief in general grace was not the same as Wesley's belief in prevenient grace, since the latter was thought to aid in people's salvation. Prevenient grace had a far more positive and constructive role, according to Wesley, that included salvation as well as the spiritual development of Christians. General grace, however, had more to do with life in this world, aiding people in restraining the immediate effects of sin and evil. Thus prevenient grace had a more dynamic and fruitful impact upon people's spiritual lives, since the Holy Spirit persistently interacts with people—leading, guiding, and empowering them to participate in spiritual growth.

Despite Wesley's emphasis on prevenient grace, it represents one of multiple ways that God's grace works in the lives of people, in general, and of believers, in particular. Although he focused mostly on their salvific implications, Wesley distinguished between the various ways in which God graciously works in the lives of people. Thus, Wesley spoke about prevenient grace, convincing grace, justifying grace, and sanctifying grace. Of course, each reference to grace signifies different functions grace plays in people's salvation. With prevenient grace, emphasis is not placed upon the cooperative role people play, but upon the need for God's gracious initiation of salvation. Thereafter, people have responsibility—graciously enabled by God—to respond in faith and repentance. Wesley said:

> Salvation is carried on by convincing grace, usually in Scripture termed repentance; which brings a larger measure of self-knowledge, and a farther deliverance from the heart of stone. Afterwards we experience the proper Christian salvation; whereby, "through grace," we "are saved by faith;" consisting of those two grand branches, justification and sanctification.[13]

Faith and repentance represent conversion, according to Wesley, and they are accompanied by God's justifying grace. By justification, people are saved from the penal effects of sin and restored to both the favor and fellowship of God. Thereafter, by sanctification—the sanctifying grace of God—believers are redeemed from the power of sin and go through a progression of restoration in the image of God. Wesley and Calvin did not disagree with regard to justification. As already stated, Wesley did not consider himself farther than a "hair's breadth" in difference from Calvin regarding the matter of justification by grace through faith. However, with regard to sanctifying grace, the two men notably disagreed. According to Wesley, grace is available preveniently for sanctification as well as justification. Christians ought to act responsibly in partaking of God's biblically prescribed means of growing in grace.

Means of Grace

Both Wesley and Calvin wrote about Christian means of grace, though they had different views of them. For Calvin, God worked the means of grace efficaciously in the lives of believers; for Wesley, God worked the means of grace preveniently with believers. In book IV of the *Institutes,* Calvin talks about "the external means or aids by which God invites us into the society of Christ and holds us therein." Sometimes these "means or aids" are referred to as "means of grace"—that is, the ways or channels through which God graciously works in people's lives, especially the lives of those who are believers. God works faith and salvation in people inwardly; yet God also works outwardly in their lives. Calvin primarily talked about how God works through the church, preaching, and sacraments. Echoing the words of the patristic Cyprian, Calvin said, "[F]or those to whom he [i.e., God] is Father the church may also be Mother."[14] He also emphasized the importance of pastor-led ministry as the way to teach people about God. In particular, pastors are appointed to preach and teach about "the heavenly doctrine."[15]

More than other means of grace, the sacraments represent "a visible word" by which God works graciously in the lives of people. Calvin said, "Augustine calls a sacrament 'a visible word' for the reason that it represents God's promises as painted in a picture and sets them before our sight, portrayed graphically and in the manner of images."[16] Calvin continued, "Or we might call them mirrors in which we may contemplate the riches of God's grace, which he lavishes upon us."[17] The sacraments are offered to everyone; however, they are only effectual through faith, as the Holy Spirit gives people an increase in grace as a kind of spiritual food.

Calvin rejected the Roman Catholic belief in seven sacraments, and only believed that two are biblical: baptism and the Lord's Supper. Baptism serves to confirm and strengthen faith, even in infant baptism. Although baptism is not required for salvation, Calvin believed that infants may receive baptism because infants should not be excluded from salvation.[18] With regard to the Lord's Supper, Calvin believed it nourished the faith of believers, strengthened their assurance, and preserved their salvation. Although the Lord's Supper is not a means of the special grace God gives for salvation, it remains a means of grace for sustaining us spiritually.

Wesley also believed in the means of grace, and considered them essential for all stages of salvation, which extend throughout Christians' lives. He said, "By 'means of grace' I understand outward signs, words, or actions ordained of God, and appointed for this end—to be the *ordinary* channels whereby he might convey to men preventing, justifying, or sanctifying grace."[19] Unlike Calvin, Wesley thought that God preveniently used the means of grace to call people to salvation as well as for working in and through them. The means of grace were not limited to the church, preaching, and sacraments, as Calvin suggested. They included a variety of ways that God intends to work graciously in people and the church. Thus, the means of grace were as important in sanctifying people as well as in justifying them.

Wesley listed the means of grace on numerous occasions. He distinguished between "instituted" and "prudential" means of grace. In his "Minutes of Several Conversations," Wesley said that the means of grace instituted by God in the Bible included the following: prayer, "searching the Scriptures," the Lord's Supper, fasting, and "Christian conference."[20] By Christian conference, Wesley emphasized accountability among Christians, which best occurred in the context of small groups. He set up an effective network of small groups that included societies that met midweek in addition to Sunday morning worship; class meetings for smaller fellowship groups; and bands that consisted of the smallest groups of Christians, usually separated by gender, who wanted daily accountability among one another for the sake of spiritual growth.

In addition to these biblically instituted means of grace, Wesley spoke of prudential (or wise) means of grace. Although these means of grace may not have been explicitly mentioned in the Bible as means per se, they represented tried-and-true methods of spiritual formation in church history as well as in people's own experiences. Most had to do with acts of mercy and charity for the poor, but there was no set number of prudential means of grace. There are many wise and beneficial practices that may be used for growth in Christian faith, hope, and love. Wesley said that such practices included "watching, denying ourselves, taking up our cross, exercise of the presence of God," and so on.[21]

Like Calvin, Wesley wanted to make it clear that such religious practices were not an end in themselves. They did not guarantee salvation, and they could actually distract us from remembering that we are saved by grace through faith. But because such means of grace were mentioned in the Bible, briefly or at length, Wesley was confident that they aided people at all stages of salvation and the Christian life.

In this regard, Wesley's emphasis on the prevenient nature of grace affirmed that God and people work—albeit mysteriously—together for their conversion, perseverance, and spiritual growth. God intends that the means of grace should include responsible action on the part of people. Such action was thought to be attributed to God's general will as well as to grace. But people are to act decisively and responsibly with regard to all spiritual matters, including biblical teachings about the means of grace. The Bible talks about such means in order that Christians may learn about them and implement them in life. They are to implement them not because of reliance upon human ability and merit for salvation, but because God revealed that the means of grace are ways that God wants to work cooperatively in relationship with people, rather than in spite of them.

Final Thoughts

Wesley and Calvin prominently placed God's grace at the center of our relationship with God. People are saved by grace through faith; it is not a matter of human work or merit. Both men completely agreed with each other that it is God who initiates, sustains, and completes people's salvation. There is never a hint of natural or human ability to deny God's sovereignty.

They disagreed with regard to how God's grace works in the lives of people. Calvin believed that divine grace works effectually—that is, that no one can ultimately resist God's will for his or her life. People cannot do anything to aid or contribute to their salvation, indeed to the whole of their lives, since God determines all that happens. Conversely, Wesley believed that God's grace facilitates people's freedom to choose or not to choose to cooperate with divine grace. God preveniently works by grace in the lives of people, making it possible for them to love God as well as to reject God. Such grace neither diminishes the sovereignty of God nor gives people responsibility apart for the empowering work of the Holy Spirit. Yet Wesley believed that prevenient grace best makes sense of the teachings, covenants, and conditions of the Bible. Although one can imagine how simple life would be if all things occurred irresistibly by the grace of God, both the Bible and experience confirm that life—both temporal and eternal—requires people to think and act in responsible ways, always cognizant that they do so by divine grace.

Discussion Questions

1. Why do you think that the hymn "Amazing Grace" continues to be so popular hundreds of years after having been written?

2. Although divine grace may, of course, work irresistibly in the lives of people, why might God want to work preveniently in relationship with them instead?

3. In what ways are the stories told by Wesley and Calvin helpful in understanding the nature of grace and how God wants to interact with people?

4. If you believe that people have a measure of freedom, made possible by the grace of God, to what extent are they free? What may restrict God's grace in our lives?

5. Contrast Wesley's belief in prevenient grace and Calvin's belief in general (or common) grace. How are they the same, and how are they different?

6. How do the various means of grace help us? Do they help only for salvation, or do they continue to help people live the Christian life? How?

Chapter 5

SALVATION: MORE UNLIMITED THAN LIMITED

For God so loved the world that he gave his only Son, so that everyone who believes in him may not perish but may have eternal life. (John 3:16)

When I was a teen, I sometimes felt intimidated by dramatic conversion stories that I heard, seemingly told on a regular basis in my Christian youth group at church. The stories usually came from popular books or movies about people who had been saved from lives of drunkenness, illegal drug use, wanton sexuality, and so on. The stories had various effects on me. On the one hand, they were sensational and caught my attention. On the other hand, the stories made me feel as if I had missed out on something—either I had missed the opportunity to experience a profligate life, or I had missed out on the opportunity to have a dramatic conversion testimony. These responses may seem silly to a reader of this book, but for a kid who had been raised in a relatively sheltered church by sheltered parents in a sheltered hometown, I felt spiritually cheated.

As I grew older and began to study Christianity more in depth, I felt better about the fact that dramatic conversion experiences probably have little to do with God blessing one person more than another. The particularities of how people experience conversion most likely have more to do with people's personality, religious background, and sociocultural context than they have to do with the quantity or quality of grace people receive from God. Since the nineteenth century, scholars such as William James have investigated people's conversion experiences and analyzed them, for example, in his book entitled *The Varieties of Religious Experience.* James concluded that the particularities of conversion or any religious experience probably have more to do with the particularities of our humanness than with inequitable spiritual relations with God.

John Wesley had a dramatic religious experience on May 24, 1738—his so-called Aldersgate experience. In his journal, Wesley described it the following way:

> In the evening I went very unwillingly to a society in Aldersgate Street, where one was reading Luther's preface to the Epistle to the Romans. About a quarter before nine, while he was describing the change which God works in the heart through faith in Christ, I felt my heart strangely warmed. I felt I did trust in Christ, Christ alone for salvation; and an assurance was given me that He had taken away my sins, even mine, and saved me from the law of sin and death.[1]

What happened to Wesley that day? Lamentably, the subject has been a matter of ongoing debate: Was Wesley converted? Did he receive assurance of salvation? Was Wesley entirely sanctified? Was it merely one of many religious experiences that Christians might have throughout their lives?

Some debate also surrounds the conversion of John Calvin. In 1533, he had a religious experience that he described in more than one way. In his *Commentary on the Book of Psalms,* Calvin said:

> God by a sudden conversion subdued and brought my mind to a teachable frame, which was more hardened in such matters than might have been expected from one at my early period of life. Having thus received some taste and knowledge of true godliness, I was immediately inflamed with so intense a desire to make progress therein, that although I did not altogether leave off other studies, yet I pursued them with less ardour.[2]

Here conversion is described as a sudden change of "mind," which produced an inflamed "desire" to live a godly life. Elsewhere Calvin described his conversion more as an emotional and arduous process that resulted in supplication for deliverance from divine judgment. According to Bruce Gordon, Calvin said:

> Being exceedingly alarmed at the misery into which I had fallen, and much more at that which threatened me in view of eternal death, I, duty bound, made it my first business to betake myself to your way, condemning my past life, not without groans and tears. And now, O Lord, what remains to a wretch like me, but instead of defence, earnestly to supplicate you not to judge that fearful abandonment of your Word according to its deserts, from which in your wondrous goodness you have at last delivered me.[3]

The religious experiences of Wesley and Calvin reveal how difficult it is to talk about salvation in a singular, definitive way. Yet, Christians testify in ways that communicate biblical teaching as well as resonate with their own experience. Although salvation represents a core teaching of both Wesley and Calvin, they understood its occurrence in notably different ways. In order to recognize those differences, we need to learn about their understanding of God's gracious provision for people's salvation, starting with the Christian doctrine of atonement.

Atonement

Both Wesley and Calvin believed that salvation occurs entirely by the grace of God. People do not earn or merit it; instead, salvation is a gift of God. How did God provide for salvation? It occurred through the life, death, and resurrection of Jesus Christ, who became incarnate and was the Messiah (Hebrew, *mashiah*, "anointed one," or Greek, *Christos*). He atoned for the sins of humanity, and through him God redeemed people and reestablishes relationship with them. The doctrine of the atonement (Old English, *at-one-ment*) summarizes Christian beliefs about how God provided salvation through Jesus and continues to save people through the presence and work of the Holy Spirit.

In church history, several views of the atonement arose. Calvin affirmed the historic doctrine of the substitutionary atonement. From this perspective, Jesus died as a substitute in place of humanity, who—on account of sin—deserved judgment and death. Calvin said: "This is our acquittal: the guilt that held us liable for punishment has been transferred to the head of the Son of God [Isa. 53:12]. We must, above all, remember this substitution, lest we tremble and remain anxious throughout life—as if God's righteous vengeance, which the Son of God has taken upon himself, still hung over us."[4] People receive the benefits of the atonement by grace through faith. Because Calvin emphasized the penal (or legal, forensic) aspect of Jesus' objective work of salvation on behalf of people, it is sometimes known as the "penal substitutionary view of the atonement."

Wesley largely agreed with the substitutionary view of the atonement. In talking about the atonement of Jesus, Wesley said, "His sufferings were the penal effects of our sins. 'The chastisement of our peace.'"[5] The point that Wesley and Calvin disagreed on had to do with the universality of Jesus' atonement, or at least the universal availability of it to people. According to Wesley, Jesus atoned "for all the sins of the whole world," not just for the elect.[6] People must still receive the benefits of the atonement by grace through faith. Not everyone responds in faith; some resist God's grace.

At this point, Wesley and Calvin disagreed. Although Calvin argued that

Jesus Christ atoned for the sin of everyone, only the elect will ever benefit from it. This suggests that Jesus may not have died as a substitute for everyone, but just for the elect. Calvin said:

> As Scripture, then, clearly shows, we say that God once established by his eternal and unchangeable plan those whom he long before determined once for all to receive into salvation, and those whom, on the other hand, he would devote to destruction. We assert that, with respect to the elect, this plan was founded upon his freely given mercy, without regard to human worth; but by his just and irreprehensible but incomprehensible judgment he has barred the door of life to those whom he has given over to damnation. Now among the elect we regard the call as a testimony of election. Then we hold justification another sign of its manifestation, until they come into the glory in which the fulfillment of that election lies. But as the Lord seals his elect by call and justification, so, by shutting off the reprobate from knowledge of his name or from the sanctification of his Spirit, he, as it were, reveals by these marks what sort of judgment awaits them.[7]

The prospect that Jesus died only for the elect is known as the "doctrine of limited atonement." Calvin did not use the phrase, but many of his followers considered it the logical implication of Calvin's theology. The doctrine of limited atonement continues to be debated among his followers. This is in part because of how Calvin should be interpreted.

Consider Calvin's commentary on John 3:16. On the one hand, Calvin said that "God shows himself to be reconciled to the whole world, when he invites all men without exception to the faith of Christ, which is nothing else than an entrance into life."[8] These words suggest an unlimited atonement; yet, Calvin followed the aforementioned quotation with the following words: "For Christ is made known and held out to the view of all, but the elect alone are they whose eyes God opens, that they may seek him by faith."[9] Thus, despite Calvin's apparent claims to the universality of Jesus Christ's atonement, only those who are elect—determined before the foundation of the world—finally benefit from it.

Wesley ardently disagreed with the implication that Jesus' atonement was in any way limited. However, in affirming the universal availability of redemption for humanity, Wesley was accused by Calvinists of universalism— that is, the belief that all people will ultimately be saved. For example, in his sermon "Free Grace," Wesley appended a hymn entitled "Universal Redemption."[10] However, the accusation of universalism misunderstands Wesley's emphasis on prevenient grace and how God graciously enables people to decide for themselves to receive salvation or to reject it. Although God universally offers salvation to people, only those who believe and repent will receive the gift of Jesus' atonement. Those who do not believe and repent in response to the gospel will not be saved; nor will they receive eternal life in heaven.

Because Calvinists rejected the possibility of anyone thwarting the will of God, the efficacy of Jesus Christ dying for everyone seemed illogical, since not everyone would be saved. Thus, they appealed to the doctrine of limited atonement to explain their belief that only the elect—those predestined by God for salvation—would receive the benefit of eternal life. Although Calvin may not have explicitly affirmed limited atonement, it was a logical implication of his system of beliefs, which his followers recognized and promoted, even if it seemed to limit Jesus' atoning work.[11]

Order of Salvation

Sometimes Christians describe the atonement as the "objective" work of God for salvation—that is, the tangible, historical guarantee of people's redemption. In response to God's work, the "subjective" work of salvation has to do with how people appropriate or experience that salvation in life. In the introduction to this chapter, I talked about the debate that surrounded the religious experiences of both Wesley and Calvin. I categorize their experiences as part of the "subjective" dimension of salvation; so it is no wonder that subjectivity and diversity characterize our understanding of how salvation may occur, or even feel, in people's experience.

In addition to the subjective dimension of salvation, debate arose in church history with regard to the *ordo salutis* (Latin, "order of salvation"). Until the time of the Reformation, not much theological effort had been given to identifying a particular order of how people are saved. For the most part, the Roman Catholic understanding of salvation ordinarily follows a sacramental view of salvation. Although Roman Catholics believe in seven sacraments, five of them have to do with salvation. Sacramentally speaking, salvation begins with the sacrament of (1) baptism, which is followed by the sacrament of (2) confirmation, at which time people affirm the Christian faith into which they have been baptized. Having reached the age of reason (or age of accountability), confirmed Christians may then partake in the sacrament of the (3) Eucharist, grow spiritually through the sacrament of (4) reconciliation, and be graciously aided in dire times by the sacrament of the (5) anointing of the sick and dying. For all practical purposes, these five sacraments ordinarily serve as the order of salvation.

After the Reformation, it became increasingly important to Protestants to identify and distinguish themselves from Roman Catholic beliefs and practices as well as to distinguish themselves from one another. However, the determination to create a stated order of salvation did not formally arise until the eighteenth century, and was begun by German Lutherans, who lived long after the time of Calvin and who were geographically as well as theologically distant from Wesley. Neither Wesley nor Calvin focused on determining a formal order of salvation. To be sure, there was an implied order of salvation in the writings of both men. For example, Wesley published a sermon entitled "The Scripture Way of Salvation," but it had more to do with advocating salvation by faith than with delineating a sequence of salvific events. In consequence, it is not appropriate to project an order of salvation upon them, even though numerous followers of Wesley and Calvin have attempted to do so.

Some approaches to determining an order of salvation are more descriptive than prescriptive. That is, they attempt to describe ordinary progressions that seem to occur in people's experience of salvation, rather than describe an invariable, dogmatic ordering. Such descriptive attempts may be helpful to people in trying to understand their salvation, spiritual growth, and how others might be saved. However, some approaches to stating an order of salvation are prescriptive. Although prescriptive approaches may sound appealing because their adherents seem certain and passionate in their promotion of a particular order of salvation, they may also be too narrow (or wide, imprecise, etc.) in their understanding and thus detrimental to those for whom ordinary life and orders of salvation do not readily apply. Not even the Bible seems to provide a normative order of salvation, since first-century people converted in different times and places, with seemingly different experiences of God's grace.

Certainly, some dimensions of salvation regularly seem to occur in the Bible as well as in Christians' understanding of salvation: grace, faith, repentance, justification, sanctification, and glorification. But other theological concepts arise that not all Christians use (or use the same way): foreknowledge, predestination, election, calling, illumination, conversion, regeneration, adoption, assurance, mystical union, perseverance, mortification, entire sanctification, and so on.

If readers are new to these terms, then take heart. The array of terms related to salvation in particular (and to theology in general) can be daunting, especially for those untutored in Christian theology. Part of me wants to give brief definitions for all of the aforementioned terms. Yet, readers must be aware that there is not necessarily consensus for how each term is defined or theologically nuanced. For example, predestination may be qualified as particular or general, and grace may be qualified as effectual or prevenient. As helpful as an order of salvation might be (and charts that illustrate orders of salvation), such orderings may be as problematic in practice (Christian life) as they are in theory (theology). Thus expectations should be tempered in how prescriptively orders of salvation are utilized theologically in discussing people's lives.

Rather than talk about formal orders of salvation in describing the theology of Wesley and Calvin, I will talk about them in more general, proximate ways. Historically, I want to avoid projecting upon Wesley and Calvin orders that do not indisputably appear in their writings. Theologically, it is still possible—and important—to talk about general orders or trajectories of salvation that observably appear in their writings, even though particularities of their respective understandings remain a matter of debate among their followers. Be that as it may, sufficient clarity in their orders of salvation is available for contrasting the different ways that Wesley and Calvin understood and promoted salvation.

Calvin's View of Salvation

Because of Calvin's strong emphasis on the sovereignty of God, salvation is—from start to finish—the work of God. When he talked about divine grace, Calvin emphasized the effectual (or irresistible) nature of God's election of those who will receive eternal life, and the reprobation of those who will receive eternal damnation. Again, he considered the predestination of people to be a great boon to them. By themselves, they have no hope whatsoever for salvation. They are sinful through and through, and it is only by God's grace, election, and predestination that some may be saved. Christians, at least, should be comforted and encouraged knowing that faith comes entirely from God, and that they have no need to worry about a salvation for which they are not ultimately responsible.

As soon as I use terms like "the decrees of God" and "election," I feel somewhat stymied by the followers of Calvin, who debate over the precise order of salvation. For example, some talk about the logical order of God's election preceding divine permission for the fall of humanity (supralapsarianism), while others talk about the logical order of God's permission for the fall of humanity preceding God's election (infralapsarianism). For the sake of this book, I will not engage the in-house debates among Calvinists. Likewise, I will not engage the in-house debates among Wesleyans with regard to a precise or standard order of salvation. Because intramural debates occur among both Calvinists and Wesleyans, I choose to speak of their orders of salvation more broadly than narrowly.

For example, union with Jesus Christ was a prominent theme in Calvin's view of salvation, but its precise place in the order of salvation has varied among his followers, if it has appeared at all. To Calvin, union with Christ involves an "indwelling of Christ in our hearts—in short, that mystical union."[12] Although he mostly talked about union with Christ in the context of the sacraments, Calvin considered it to occur prior to people's justification and sanctification. Union with Christ makes possible the imputed righteousness people receive by means of Jesus' atonement. It guarantees the effectual calling of people to salvation, which also enables their regeneration, faith, and repentance.

Justification by Grace through Faith

Without doubt, Calvin's view of justification represents the most prominent emphasis in his view of salvation. People are justified by grace through faith, which reflects the Reformation emphases upon *sola gratia* and *sola fide.* People are justified, and righteousness is imputed to them. With his juridical approach to theology, Calvin considered Paul's teachings on justification to be the best way to clarify how God redeems people. He said, "Therefore, we explain justification simply as the acceptance with which God receives us into his favor as righteous men. And we say that it consists in the remission of sins and the imputation of Christ's righteousness."[13] Calvin continued:

> Therefore, "to justify" means nothing else than to acquit of guilt him who was accused, as if his innocence were confirmed. Therefore, since God justifies us by the intercession of Christ, he absolves us not by the confirmation of our own innocence but by the imputation of righteousness, so that we who are not righteous in ourselves may be reckoned as such in Christ.[14]

The imputation of Jesus' righteousness has to do with how God now views us "as if" we are righteous, since God accepts his righteousness in our stead. People who are elect may remain sinners, but they are forgiven on account of the atoning work of Jesus. Finally, it must always be remembered that people's justification occurs as a gift and never as a work. Calvin said, "The power of justifying, which faith possesses, does not lie in any worth of works. Our justification rests upon God's mercy alone and Christ's merit."[15]

Those who are justified enjoy additional works of God's grace in their lives. They experience sanctification and the spirit of adoption as children of God. Calvin said:

> To prove the first point—that God justifies not only by pardoning but by regenerating—he asks whether God leaves as they were by nature those whom he justifies, changing none of their vices. This is exceedingly easy to answer: as Christ cannot be torn into parts, so these two which we perceive in him together and conjointly are inseparable—namely, righteousness and sanctification. Whomever, therefore, God receives into grace, on them he at

the same time bestows the spirit of adoption [Rom. 8:15], by whose power he remakes them to his own image.[16]

Calvin emphasized sanctification more than did Luther; that is, Calvin emphasized how God wants to nurture believers into greater spiritual maturity, greater Christlikeness. Both Calvin and Luther believed that sanctification as well as justification occurred by grace through faith. But Calvin argued that the Bible talks much about the Christian life and how believers ought to live in accordance with the third use of the law—the moral use—for their mortification and vivification, which were terms he used to describe sanctification. Of course, Calvin's view of sanctification differed from that of Wesley, which is why the next chapter is devoted to its discussion under the topic of spirituality.

Calvin believed that those who are chosen by God—the elect—will persevere until the time of their final glorification. Like justification, the perseverance of Christians is a gift of God. Calvin said: "There is no other reason why some persevere to the end, while others fall at the beginning of the course. For perseverance itself is indeed also a gift of God, which he does not bestow on all indiscriminately, but imparts to whom he pleases."[17] Calvin continued, "Only his elect does he [i.e., God] account worthy of receiving the living root of faith so that they may endure to the end."[18] Augustine talked about the perseverance of the saints, as did Calvin's followers. Other phrases used to capture the surety of salvation have been popularly referred to as "eternal security" or "once saved, always saved." These terms are not found in Calvin, and caution should be used in attributing them to him. But they suggest the notion that if people have faith, then they likely have it because God endued faith in them, and they cannot resist God's election.

Wesley's View of Salvation

Although Wesley and Calvin shared many similarities in their views of salvation, they differ with regard to the work of God's grace in the order of salvation. From Calvin's perspective, grace works effectually (or irresistibly). It is limited to those who are elect, namely those predestined for salvation. Indeed those who are reprobate—those predetermined for damnation—neither do nor can receive eternal life on account of God's will, which decrees (or determines) everyone's eternal state. In contrast to Calvin, Wesley argued for the universal or unlimited prevenient work of God's grace. That is, God initiates salvation in everyone by grace, and continues by enabling people to have the opportunity to decide for themselves whether to accept or reject God's gift of salvation.

The fact that people universally receive prevenient grace verifies that God wants everyone to be saved. The fact that some are not saved is because they have freely rejected God; it is not a matter of a predetermined plan that God established before the foundation of the world. God may foreknow the future and predetermine in general the conditions of life, but God does not predetermine in particular people's salvation or damnation. The difference between Calvin's view of grace working effectually and Wesley's view of grace working preveniently cannot be overemphasized. It exemplifies other differences between Wesley and Calvin with regard to the order of salvation.

According to Wesley, prevenient grace makes possible the call of God for people to believe and repent—to convert to Jesus Christ and the gospel of salvation. God foreknows those who will believe and repent, and predestines their election, based upon that which God knows throughout eternity. God foreknows, predestines, calls, convinces, justifies, and glorifies. This order does not encapsulate the whole of salvation, but it illustrates how God works in people for their justification—for how God redeems people from sin and judgment.

Let us consider a sermon in which Wesley agreed with Calvin's emphasis on salvation by grace through faith. The very first sermon listed in his collection of sermons was entitled "Salvation by Faith." In it, Wesley said:

> If then sinful man find favour with God, it is "grace upon grace!" ... If God vouchsafe still to pour fresh blessings upon us—yea, the greatest of all blessings, salvation—what can we say to these things but "Thanks be unto God for his unspeakable gift!" And thus it is. Herein "God commendeth his love toward us, in that, while we were yet sinners, Christ died" to save us. "By grace," then, "are ye saved through faith." Grace is the source, faith the condition, of salvation.[19]

The issue that Wesley and Calvin disagreed on had to do with whether faith represented a condition or result of salvation—of God's gracious work in people for their redemption. From Calvin's perspective, faith represented evidence of God's effectual grace; whereas from Wesley's perspective, faith represented evidence of God's prevenient grace. Wesley thought that the Bible maintains faith as a condition of salvation, which God foreknows. In fact, he argued that Calvin and his followers emphasized God's absolute predestination so much that they jeopardized the biblical doctrine of salvation by faith. If election is unconditional and if atonement is limited, then people's faith becomes irrelevant, since God decreed who is saved and who is damned before anyone was even born. Wesley said, "[T]hose who maintain absolute predestination, who hold decrees that have no condition at all, cannot be consistent with themselves, unless they deny salvation by faith, as well as salvation by works."[20]

God's grace works preveniently to call people to salvation, to convince them of the need to repent, and then to justify them. But for Wesley, justification was not the entirety of salvation. On the contrary, it was the beginning of a dynamic opportunity for relationship with God and growth into Christlikeness. God's grace regenerates people as well as justifies them, which leads to both assurance (at least initial) and greater convincing of ongoing sin in their lives. Ordinarily, it is not until after the time of conversion that believers become aware of their need of further blessing from God, facilitated by God's sanctifying grace as performed by the person and work of the Holy Spirit. Indeed, Wesley was quite hopeful about the degree to which God's Spirit may bless people with regard to the perseverance and assurance of their salvation, and to their sanctification.

Both Calvin and Wesley emphasized sanctification, but Wesley is often distinguished for his view of it. In his sermon "The Scripture Way of Salvation," Wesley talked about the nature of salvation, which "consists of two general parts, justification and sanctification."[21] For the most part, Wesley agreed with the Protestant reformers with regard to justification by faith. The point they disagreed on, with regard to salvation holistically understood, was the dynamic of how God wants to continue working graciously and preveniently in the lives of believers so that they cooperate with the Holy Spirit in their spiritual growth. This is why Wesley talked about entire sanctification, since he believed that the God of the universe, who has the power to heal and perform miracles, wants to accomplish amazing transformation in Christians. If God is thought to be perfect, then to what other goal would God lead Christians other than to greater perfection in Christlikeness, in love, and in ministry?

Assurance of Salvation

One final point of difference between Wesley and Calvin with regard to their views of salvation has to do with the assurance of salvation. Calvin believed that, if people are saved, then they are certain of it. He said, "Briefly, he alone is truly a believer who, convinced by a firm conviction that God is a kindly and well-disposed Father toward him, promises himself all things on the basis of his generosity; who, relying upon the promises of divine benevolence toward him, lays hold on an undoubted expectation of salvation."[22] Calvin's confidence was based on his doctrine of predestination and on the objective work of Jesus Christ for our atonement. He did not think that one is justified without being sure of it. Our experience of faith, good works, and indeed the Holy Spirit may aid our sense of assurance, but they are secondary, at best, and misleading, at worst. With regard to good works, Calvin cautioned, "From this it comes about that his conscience feels more fear and consternation than assurance."[23] Calvin was not unsympathetic to those who doubted their salvation, and thought that people's good works and other religious experiences might encourage them. But people's assurance of salvation and their perseverance relied more upon their faith in the objective work (and promise) of the atonement, as found in the Bible, than upon any subjective experience of it.

The dynamic of living in an ever-transforming relationship with Jesus Christ was at the heart of Calvin's break with Luther over law and gospel. For Calvin, the third use of the law is the law's ongoing purpose for believers. He would not sanction using predestination (and election) as a pretext to justify inaction in the life of faith. Conversely, the knowledge of election is always a personal, eschatological matter; it is to encourage believers that their progression in living in Christ is a sign of being a child of God. But assurance of election is never a *fait accompli,* since one's election in Christ is always provisional until this mortal life is over.

Subsequent followers of Calvin thought that he had been too severe in his teachings about assurance of salvation, thinking he may have argued too strongly that no one could be certain of his or her salvation, since no subjective or personal evidence was reliable. Although one may have great hope in the biblical promises of salvation for those who believe, the Bible also talks about the benefits of life in the Spirit, which bring progressive hope in the believer with regard to the prospect of eternal life after temporal death. Later Calvinists were more upbeat about the assurance of salvation that people may experience, for example, as found in The Westminster Confession.[24] But Calvin did not think that assurance of salvation represented a kind of religious experience subsequent to conversion. Instead people should turn to the promises of God's salvation as found in the Bible, emphasizing the priority of faith in such promises, which represent the only sure evidence of eternal life.

Wesley believed strongly in the assurance of salvation. He talked about both direct and indirect witnesses to it. In addition to the promises of the Bible, Wesley appealed to the witness of the Holy Spirit in Romans 8:15-17. He said, "By 'the testimony of the Spirit' I mean an inward impression of the soul, whereby the Spirit of God immediately and directly witnesses to my spirit that I am a child of God, that Jesus Christ hath loved me, and given himself for me; that all my sins are blotted out, and I, even I, am reconciled to God."[25] This sense of assurance is a privilege or blessing that Christians may experience, though some remain ignorant of it. Wesley was not afraid to talk about the experiential dimensions of Christianity. God's salvation permeates all of life. Certainly people need to be discerning, since experiences can be misleading, but the experience of salvation touches upon people's heart, soul, and strength as well as mind. As Christians grow in relationship with God, they become more attuned to the presence and blessings of God's Spirit.

Wesley lived during the Enlightenment era, and his emphases on religious experience were often met with accusations of enthusiasm—a pejorative term that applied to enthusiastic worship practices as well as theological suspicion. However, Wesley thought that assurance had to do with more than cognitive affirmation of the promises of the Bible, as encouraging as they may be. After all, people are saved by becoming personally reconciled with God, mediated by the Holy Spirit, and experience adoption as children of God. As such, progress proceeds from the "faith of a servant" of God to that of a child of God who receives benefits of assurance superior to those of lesser faith. [26] Wesley considered his doctrine of assurance to be one of the great teachings of Methodism. He considered it "one grand part of the testimony which God has given [the Methodists] to bear to all mankind."[27]

In addition to the direct witness of the Holy Spirit, Wesley talked about indirect witnesses. They include a good conscience and the fruit of the Spirit. Such witnesses contribute to degrees of assurance, because not everyone experiences assurance of salvation at the time of conversion. Indeed people commonly experience questions and doubts, but the Holy Spirit works to assure them both directly and indirectly that they are indeed saved, children of God.

Final Thoughts

Wesley and Calvin represent strong advocates of the Protestant emphasis upon salvation by grace through faith. It is a gift that Jesus Christ merited on behalf of humanity through his life, death, and resurrection. Through Jesus' atonement, salvation is made available as a substitution on behalf of we who are sinful.

Although Calvin did not claim that Jesus Christ's atonement was limited per se, it is certainly true that Calvin believed that God effectually saves only some people. They are saved because God unconditionally elects (determines or predetermines) those who receive eternal life; God also reprobates those who will receive eternal damnation. Calvin considered God's sovereign control over the eternal states of people to be a great comfort, since no one by himself or herself can earn or merit salvation. However, Wesley considered Calvin's views to be mistaken. Instead, Wesley argued that Jesus clearly died on behalf of everyone; the atonement was not limited. Not all people will be saved; those who freely choose to reject God's offer of salvation will be judged for their sins. Yet, those who believe—by the grace of God—will be saved, since faith represents the condition for eternal life. According to Wesley, salvation involves a restored relationship with God, and God intends that people choose to be reconciled.

Discussion Questions

1. What is your understanding of the atonement of Jesus Christ? In what way did his life, death, and resurrection provide for our salvation?

2. What do you think about the concept of an order of salvation? In what ways may an order of salvation be helpful, and in what ways may it be unhelpful?

3. Why was Calvin so encouraged to believe that salvation occurred by the sovereignty of God's gracious initiation alone? What is the danger of believing that people may somehow earn or merit eternal life?

4. What are the benefits of Wesley's belief that Jesus Christ's atonement was unlimited? What does it mean when Christians say that all may be saved?

5. In what sense do you believe that people are saved by faith? To what degree is faith credited to God, or to what degree is faith credited to people's choices?

6. What does assurance of salvation mean to you? To what degree may people—in this life—experience it? What does either Wesley or Calvin say that encourages you?

Chapter 6

Spirituality: More Holiness Than Mortification

May the God of peace himself sanctify you entirely; and may your spirit and soul and body be kept sound and blameless at the coming of our Lord Jesus Christ.
(1 Thessalonians 5:23)

When I was doing graduate studies at Princeton Theological Seminary, I became acquainted with a group of students with whom I socialized and became good friends. We would get together on a weekly basis at meals in the cafeteria, hang out late after hours of study, and sometimes go to entertainment events together. We shared with one another about our studies, futures, and other personal matters.

One woman in our group went home many weekends. I will call her Jane, though that was not her name. One week Jane informed us that she did not really go home on weekends. Instead she visited the academic institution from which she had graduated the previous year. There Jane would meet a male professor with whom she had had and continued to have a romantic affiliation. The professor apparently was married and had children, and Jane's sexual relationship with him was a secret. About every other weekend, Jane would travel in order to meet her ex-professor and carry on the extramarital affair.

However, the affair was becoming burdensome to Jane for a variety of reasons, and she wanted our advice. Because the affair—as well as the purpose for her weekend travels—was news to our group of friends, we needed more background information. Jane said that she was exhausted from the travel,

72

the time, the secrecy, the guilt, and the shame. She said that everything was weighing heavily on her.

Members of our group, including me, tried to be as empathetic and supportive of Jane as possible. But I could not help wondering about the appropriateness of her affair. Although I heard Jane talk about the practicalities of sustaining the affair, given all the emotional, financial, and academic logistics involved, I did not hear her consider the possibility of ending it. At one point—perhaps naively—I asked whether she thought that her affair was the right thing to be doing. In other words, did Jane think that she was doing anything wrong by having a sexual relationship with a married man who had been her professor?

Jane responded immediately by saying that she definitely considered herself and her ex-professor to be involved in that which was sin. She was very candid about saying that her secret relationship was biblically wrong and damaging to many, regardless of their current awareness of the relationship. So I asked Jane, that if she believed she was acting sinfully and did not see long-term reasons to continue the affair, then why did she not terminate the relationship? Jane's response was matter-of-fact: she could not end the affair because she believed it was her lot in life that she be in the relationship with her ex-professor. God understood. From her perspective, the affair was unavoidable since people are totally depraved; people cannot avoid sinning. Jane's affair just happened to be her particular weakness—her persistent temptation and indulgence—over which she had no control. It seemed inconceivable to Jane to end the affair; she could only manage it in a way that was less tumultuous spiritually, emotionally, and financially, and in ways that helped her fulfill other responsibilities. From Jane's perspective, all people face temptations and sins over which they have no decisive control. So the Christian response is to do damage control, suppressing the worst effects of sin and creating as much order in life as possible.

It is possible, in talking about Jane, that I have caricatured her life and decisions. But her resigned approach is an attitude that I have encountered in the lives of other people I have since met who seem to me to have little hope about an improved future. In Jane's understanding, since everyone is thought to sin in thought, word, and deed, including Christians, then we should expect that life has more to do with avoiding the worst of possible outcomes than with pursuing the best of possible outcomes. It did not help, in my opinion, that Jane was pursuing ordination in the Presbyterian Church. Her understanding of Presbyterian theology—influenced by Calvinistic beliefs and values—seemed to reinforce Jane's resignation to a life of sin and to getting by as best she could. Of course, it can be argued that Jane totally misunderstood both Calvin and Presbyterianism; but it can also be argued that such influences contributed to her sense of resignation to the unavoidability of sin. (I prefer to think that Jane misunderstood Calvin. But Wesley repeatedly argued that the Calvinism with which he was familiar was susceptible to antinomianism or "anti-law-ism"—that is, the belief that Christians are exempt from moral law on account of the gospel dispensation of grace.)

I grew up with a much different Christian worldview. No doubt there were many factors that influenced my hopefulness with regard to the possibility of confronting and overcoming sinful thoughts, words, and actions that I did not want. It may have included my personal temperament, my parental upbringing, and other sociocultural influences. But one constructive influence certainly had to do with my Wesleyan and Methodist background. Wesley, after all, was hopeful with regard to the degree that God's grace may work to transform people spiritually and in other ways. That hopefulness was not limited merely to individualistic growth but also to the ways in which Christians relate with others, one-on-one and societally.

Christian Spirituality

Spirituality generally has to do with the spiritual well-being and growth of Christians. The Bible offers a variety of ways in which true believers become more intimate in their relationship with God and flourish in the different dimensions of their spiritual lives. The coming of Jesus Christ, of course, was pivotal for their redemption, and the Holy Spirit continues to work in their lives until they receive the fullness of heavenly glory in eternity.

In church history, spirituality was conceived and practiced in different ways. It would be difficult to argue that one way only encapsulates the whole of the Christian life as described in the Bible. Some elements are regularly found, for example, prayer, worship, and so on. But particularities in the understanding and practice of Christian spirituality are undeniably diverse. For example, some traditions have been more evangelical, while others have been more sacramental or contemplative. Still other traditions have approached Christian spirituality through concentrated study of the Bible, holy living, social activism, or the gifts of the Holy Spirit.

Theologically, Christian spirituality has been understood in the context of sanctification—that is, belief about what happens in the lives of Christians after their conversion. Protestant reformers such as Calvin spoke often of justification, which refers to the juridical redemption of people. They also spoke of regeneration, which refers to the transformative redemption of people, usually thought to be foundational for their sanctification. But what does

74

sanctification look like? To what degree are people sanctified? How does it occur? To what degree is sanctification the responsibility of God, and to what degree are Christians responsible for it? How entirely sanctified, holy, or perfect should one expect to become?

Calvin certainly believed in sanctification. As already mentioned, some scholars say that one of the more distinctive differences between Luther and Calvin was that the latter had a far more focused and lively understanding of sanctification. Calvin did not think that the laws of God, for example, were only for the two uses that Luther described: (1) evangelical and (2) civil uses. The laws of God served a third use, a moral use, which instructed believers in how they should live subsequent to conversion. Calvin said, "Now it will not be difficult to decide the purpose of the whole law: the fulfillment of righteousness to form human life to the archetype of divine purity."[1]

Wesley is also well known for his view of sanctification. But as can be expected, Calvin and he differed with regard to the nature and extent of sanctification. Thus it will be necessary to take time in order to explore the various ways in which they understood the Christian life and how God intends for people to develop in Christlikeness.

Mortification and Vivification

After conversion, Calvin believed that God both "mortified" and "vivified" believers, which describe essential aspects of the Christian life. After repentance, God mortifies converts so that they remember they are saved by grace alone, and God consoles (or vivifies) them so that they may have hope of sharing in Jesus Christ's resurrection. Calvin said:

> But certain men well versed in penance, even long before these times, meaning to speak simply and sincerely according to the rule of Scripture, said that it consists of two parts: mortification and vivification. Mortification they explain as sorrow of soul and dread conceived from the recognition of sin and the awareness of divine judgment. . . . Furthermore, when he is touched by any sense of the judgment of God (for the one straightway follows the other) he then lies stricken and overthrown; humbled and cast down he trembles; he becomes discouraged and despairs. This is the first part of repentance, commonly called "contrition." "Vivification" they understand as the consolation that arises out of faith. That is, when a man is laid low by the consciousness of sin and stricken by the fear of God, and afterward looks to the goodness of God—to his mercy, grace, salvation, which is through Christ—he raises himself up, he takes heart, he recovers courage, and as it were, returns from death to life.[2]

These dual works of mortification and vivification are, properly speaking, the works of God and not of people. According to Calvin, "Satan tempts that he may destroy, condemn, confound, cast down, but God, that by proving his own children he may make trial of their sincerity, and establish their strength by exercising it; that he may mortify, purify, and cauterize their flesh, which unless it were forced under this restraint would play the wanton and vaunt itself beyond measure."[3]

In trying to describe Calvin's view of sanctification, it is again helpful to appeal to the theological concept of the *complexio oppositorium* (Latin, "complexity of opposites"). On the one hand, Calvin said that sanctification, including mortification and vivification, is a gift—*beneficium,* similar to what Luther said. As such, sanctification does not require human obedience—*sacrificium,* similar to what Roman Catholics said. On the other hand, Calvin did not want to say that Christians have no active role to exercise in bringing about the sanctifying work of grace in their lives. Christians are not totally passive, since they ought to live out their lives of repentance and regeneration as a function of being in Jesus Christ. It is a mystery brought to effect by faith in hearing Scripture, by being drawn by the inner witness of the Holy Spirit to share in the resurrected life of Christ, and by sharing the twin benefits of that union: mortification and vivification.

Prayer represents one of the prime duties of Christians. On the one hand, prayer is a gift through which God's providence and power are revealed.[4] On the other hand, it is a duty in which Christians should persevere. Prayer is a "duty of piety," and through it Christians experience many of the benefits spirituality.[5] For example, Calvin talked about several benefits of prayer:

> First, that our hearts may be fired with a zealous and burning desire ever to seek, love, and serve him.... Secondly, that there may enter our hearts no desire and no wish at all of which we should make him a witness.... Thirdly, that we be prepared to receive his benefits with true gratitude of heart and thanksgiving.... Fourthly, moreover, that, having obtained what we were seeking, and being convinced that he has answered our prayers, we should be led to meditate upon his kindness more ardently. And fifthly, that at the time we embrace with greater delight those things which we acknowledge to have been obtained by prayers. Finally, that use and experience may, according to the measure of our feebleness, confirm his providence.[6]

Most of Calvin's prayers were spoken publicly, but he also encouraged private prayer. Such prayers contributed to the vivification of Christians in addition to their mortification.

Although God mortifies Christians, they are to mortify themselves as well. The sanctification of believers, in fact, embraces the importance of ongoing self-denial through mortification. Because of believers' union with Jesus Christ, they ought to die to sin by mortifying themselves inwardly as well as outwardly. Calvin said:

> If our sanctification consists in mortifying our own will, then a very close correspondence appears between the outward sign and the inward reality. We must be wholly at rest that God may work in us; we must yield our will; we must resign our heart; we must give up all our fleshly desires. In short, we must rest from all activities of our own contriving so that, having God working in us [Heb. 13:21], we may repose in him [Heb. 4:9], as the apostle also teaches.[7]

Mortification emphasizes how believers may minimize the effects of sin in their lives as they suppress ongoing sin, temptation, and other evil influences that continue in their lives. Like Luther, Calvin believed that believers are "always saved, always sinners." Calvin said:

> Accordingly, we say that the old man was so crucified [Rom. 6:6], and the law of sin [cf. Rom. 8:2] so abolished in the children of God, that some vestiges remain; not to rule over them, but to humble them by the consciousness of their own weakness. And we, indeed, admit that these traces are not imputed, as if they did not exist; but at the same time we contend that this comes to pass through the mercy of God, so that the saints—otherwise deservedly sinners and guilty before God—are freed from this guilt.[8]

People are justified by faith, and they are no longer guilty of sin, because of the atonement of Jesus. But they continue to struggle for various reasons because of the power of sin as well as other powers—natural and supernatural. *Struggle,* in fact, is the very term Calvin used to describe the Christian life that people should realistically expect. Calvin said: "[W]e conclude that in this life we are to seek and hope for nothing but struggle; when we think of our crown, we are to raise our eyes to heaven. For this we must believe: that the mind is never seriously aroused to desire and ponder the life to come unless it be previously imbued with contempt for the present life."[9]

So, God has given us the promise of heaven, by means of Jesus' imputed righteousness. But we ought not to expect an untroubled life, since we struggle with sin and God continues to mortify us through various means. As Christians mortify themselves as well, they help to bring greater uprightness and order to their present lives until God puts all things right in eternity.

Of course, by living lives of self-denial, Christians are able to perform the "works of love" that tangibly demonstrate love for others.[10] Although Calvin emphasized salvation by grace through faith, he expected works of love to be paired with it. As a consequence, Christians will love their neighbor. Such works, of course, do not earn or merit salvation. But neither are they opposed to grace. Calvin said:

> From this it appears that the word "to work" is not opposed to grace but refers to endeavor.... Once they are, by knowledge of the gospel and illumination of the Holy Spirit, called into the fellowship of Christ, eternal life begins in them. Now that God has begun a good work in them, it must also be made perfect until the Day of the Lord Jesus [Phil. 1:6]. It is, however, made perfect when, resembling their Heavenly Father in righteousness and holiness, they prove themselves sons true to their nature.[11]

God uses trials and afflictions here and now, which God ordains for the purpose of Christians' sanctification. Calvin said, "For the Lord proves his people by no light trials, and does not softly exercise them, but often drives them to extremity, and allows them, so driven, to lie a long time in the mire before he gives them any taste of his sweetness."[12] Such providences of God are thought to provide grace to believers in order that the elect should, again, remember that they are in union with Jesus Christ; that they are being transformed in accord with God's plan; and that they should rejoice, knowing that all circumstances are ultimately on account of God's will, including many trials and tests. As Calvin said, "[I]t is not without cause that the Lord daily tests his elect [Gen. 22:1; Deut. 8:2; 13:3. Vg.], chastising them by disgrace, poverty, tribulation, and other sorts of affliction."[13]

From Calvin's perspective, Romans 7:14-25 represents the expected Christian life. It contains Paul's discussion about the things he wants to do that he does not do, and the things he does not want to do that he does do. For centuries Christians have debated over whether this passage pertains to the life of unregenerate people or whether it pertains to the life of regenerate, saved people. Calvin even mentioned that Augustine originally thought that the verses pertained to unbelievers; however, Augustine changed his mind. Like Augustine, Calvin believed that Romans 7:14-25 described the Christian life and how we should expect "perpetual conflict." He said:

> Now, because that depravity of nature does not so readily appear in secular man (who indulges his own desires without fear of God), Paul takes his example from a regenerated man, that is, himself. He therefore says that he has a perpetual conflict with the vestiges of his flesh, and that he is held bound in miserable bondage, so that he cannot consecrate himself wholly to obedience to the divine law [Rom. 7:18-23]. Hence, he is compelled to exclaim with groaning: "Wretched man that I am! Who will deliver me from this body subject to death?" [Rom. 7:24 p.].[14]

These experiences are thought to be helpful for believers, lest they forget that they are saved by grace and think that they have done some things worthy of God's beneficence. Of believers, Calvin said, "Yet they do not obtain full possession of freedom so as to feel no more annoyance from their flesh, but there still remains in them a continuing occasion for struggle whereby they may be exercised; and not only be exercised, but also better learn their own weakness."[15] In his opinion, Calvin thought that Christians ought to live humble lives, and that mortification helps to keep them humbly aware of their weakness, because of unending struggle.

Calvin systematically located the trajectory of sanctification within God's intent, via providence and redemption, to effect the renewal (or revitalization) of the image of God in humanity by bringing about a new humanity. The dullness of the sense of the divine in which we were fashioned to live in relationship with God is transformed into a life of ever-developing and maturing vivification of our fallen nature. Believers are renewed through the redemptive activity of the word of God effecting union between Jesus Christ and them, through faith and love, and with the hope of full renewal in God's timing. Hence, all struggles with sin are temporal in the pilgrimage of the believer.

In contrast, Wesley thought that Romans 7:14-25 describes an unregenerate person, and that Romans 8 presents a victorious resolution to the spiritual struggle of Romans 7, culminating in the words of Romans 8:37: "No, in all these things we are more than conquerors through him who loved us." Calvin was well aware of this alternative interpretation, but he considered it spiritually dangerous—"indeed monstrous"—to think that some degree of holiness or perfection of a spiritual (or moral) nature is attainable in this life.[16] On the contrary, Calvin thought that all talk of perfection, holiness, and victorious Christian living was contrary to the evidence of both the Bible and experience. Thus, such talk was to be avoided, lest Christians be tempted to believe that they had somehow contributed to their justification or sanctification.

Mortification of oneself is not a one-time activity; it is to be ongoing, a lifestyle. Calvin said, "[B]ut we may more truly say that the life of a Christian man is a continual effort and exercise in the mortification of the flesh, till it is utterly slain, and God's Spirit reigns in us."[17] Can God's Spirit reign in us? Yes, it is true that believers are saved and God views them as holy, on account of Jesus Christ's imputed righteousness. But, according to Calvin, it is not true that believers are saved—in this life—from struggle.

What Calvin had to say about sanctification, of course, only applies to those who are elect. The reprobate have no hope of justification, much less sanctification. So the benefits of sanctification only occur within the lives of the elect. Calvin said: "But as a persuasion of God's fatherly love is not deeply rooted in the reprobate, so do they not perfectly reciprocate his love as sons, but behave like hirelings. For that Spirit of love was given to Christ alone on the condition that he instill it in his members. And surely that saying of Paul's is confined to the elect."[18] In this life, baptism represents a "token of mortification," symbolizing how God works both to mortify and vivify new believers: "And, just as the twig draws substance and nourishment from the root to which it is grafted, so those who receive baptism with right faith truly feel the effective working of Christ's death in the mortification of their flesh, together with the working of his resurrection in the vivification of the Spirit [Rom. 6:8]."[19] Even with regard to infants, infant baptism symbolizes "the mortification of their corrupt and defiled nature, a mortification that they would afterward practice in mature years." [20]

People are saved by grace through faith; it is a gift and not the result of work. Likewise, if it is God's will for believers to grow spiritually and become more mature, sanctified people, then God will bring the increase. However, people are to recognize humbly that spiritual matters are because of God and not because of them. They are to praise God, and give glory and thanks to God, for both their justification and sanctification. If God brings increase, then it is because of God and not because of anything that people think, say, or do. Their mortification is both a gift from God and a task that believers are to perform, but not with the expectation that they have contributed anything toward the spiritual increase—to their vivification. Since vivification as well as sanctification in general is the work of God, the only work that believers are to be concerned with is their mortification. Although mortification may be difficult to accomplish in life, it has more to do with faithful obedience to God than it has to do with any expectation of contributing to believers' sanctification. But the self-denial of mortification does help to order life here and now in the midst of so much sinfulness and moral depravity, and it helps suppress discomforting circumstances in life and bring about greater orderliness.

Holiness and the Christian Life

Wesley had a different understanding of the Christian life and of the sanctification to which God calls believers. He was far more hopeful, more expectant, with regard to the ways in which Christians may pursue "means of grace," which God established in the Bible, and by which they may grow spiritually. Always by God's grace, believers may pursue the holiness to which God calls them, knowing that they may "plant" and "water" with spiritual disciplines and that God gives the "increase" (1 Corinthians 3:5-9). After all, throughout the Bible, God calls people to be holy. By grace, God imputes holiness through the death and resurrection of Jesus Christ, but God also commands believers to be holy as God is holy. 1 Peter 1:13-16 says:

> Therefore prepare your minds for action; discipline yourselves; set all your hope on the grace that Jesus Christ will bring you when he is revealed. Like obedient children, do not be conformed to the desires that you formerly had in ignorance. Instead, as he who call you is holy, be holy yourselves in all your conduct; for it is written, "You shall be holy, for I am holy" [quoting Leviticus 11:44-45; cf. 19:2, 20:7].

What is holiness but love? In particular, holiness has to do with love for God and neighbor. When asked about the greatest command, Jesus responded with a twofold charge:

> One of the scribes came near and heard them disputing with one another, and seeing that he answered them well, he asked him, "Which command-ment is the first of all?" Jesus answered, "The first is, 'Hear, O Israel: the Lord our God, the Lord is one; you shall love the Lord your God with all your heart, and with all your soul, and with all your mind, and with all your strength.' The second is this, 'You shall love your neighbor as yourself.' There is no other commandment greater than these." (Mark 12:28-31)

This charge was not given as an unachievable goal, according to Wesley, but an achievable objective, by the grace of God, through the presence and work of the Holy Spirit. If God is a God of miracles, after all, then Christians need not look forward to a life of futile spiritual struggle but hopefully to spiritual successes. Although Wesley did not believe that people achieved absolute per-fection in this life, they may consistently partner with God's grace in becom-ing more loving; more holy; more like Jesus. It is the work of the Holy Spirit to empower Christians and to impart righteousness to those who consecrate their lives to the lordship of Jesus.

In justification, God imputes righteousness because of the atoning work of Jesus Christ; in sanctification, God imparts righteousness because of the sanctifying work of the Holy Spirit. (Initial sanctification occurs with people's regeneration.) Just as God conditions the imputation of righteousness by the decisiveness of people's faith, God conditions the impartation of righteous-ness by the decisiveness of people's faith, both enabled by God's prevenient grace. Wesley referred to this progression in salvation as including convinc-ing, justifying, and sanctifying grace.

Wesley understood the problems involved with affirming any type of Christian perfection in this life. However, from his perspective, the com-mands of Jesus Christ were clear. In the Sermon on the Mount, Jesus said:

"Be perfect, therefore, as your heavenly Father is perfect" (Matthew 5:48). Of course, in discussion about becoming perfect, Wesley spoke both about obedience to Jesus' teachings and about perfection in love. Perfection in love, after all, represents the pinnacle of holiness, of Christlikeness. To be sure, it is far easier to disregard Matthew 5:48, consider it a goal (or ideal) that inspires but is unreachable, or project its applicability into the far future—but certainly not for life here and now. Yet Wesley believed that, in some biblical sense, God wants to disciple people into greater Christlikeness, which means growth toward perfection of holy love, rather than toward mediocrity or futility—spiritually, morally, and in relations with others.

Despite what some people might think, Wesley was realistic about the Christian life. For example, he talked about ways in which people would not become perfect. They would not become like God, or even Adam, as Wesley understood the goodness in which people were created. He said, "There is no such perfection in this life, as implies...a freedom from ignorance, mistake, temptation, connected with flesh and blood."[21] Despite challenges that occur in conceiving of the Christian life too optimistically, Wesley thought that there were greater challenges that occur in conceiving of the Christian life too pessimistically, too resignedly, and too passively. In his opinion, Calvin placed too little emphasis on the gracious outcome that may occur through people's faithful obedience to the laws of God and God's divinely appointed means of grace.

Although Calvin emphasized the need for obedience, it did not occur with the hope of God using such obedience to add in believers' spiritual formation. Without that hope, Wesley thought that believers might become complacent or despair about sanctification, the prospect of spiritual formation, and obedience to the laws of God. Complacency about the law may result in antinomian disregard for the laws of God. And Wesley feared that Calvinism tempted people with antinomianism, since so little importance was placed upon people's responsibility for pursuing Christlikeness. Moreover, without hope of growth in grace, Christians may lose heart about empowerment for holy living, available to them through the Holy Spirit, subsequent to justification.

From Wesley's perspective, there should be no "half a Christian"—that is, one who receives justification by faith but fails to go on toward sanctification by faith.[22] In other places, Wesley contrasted the faith of a "servant of God" from that of a "child of God."[23] The faith of a servant results in justification; the faith of a child—a son or daughter of God—results in justification, assurance of salvation, and sanctification that increases as both God and believers partner through the means of grace.

Indeed Wesley was hopeful—even optimistic—about the ways in which God graciously works in the lives of believers, exhorting them to partner with the Holy Spirit in becoming more holy; more Christlike; more loving. To be sure, life would still be filled with questions, problems, and even catastrophes of one nature or another—inside a person as well as outside them. Wesley had no Pollyanna approach to the Christian life. But he was steadfastly hopeful because he considered the grace of God to be superior to the power of sin, evil, and Satan. So much so was this the case that Wesley talked about Christian perfection, or what he also called "entire sanctification."

Entire Sanctification

Wesley wrote a book entitled *A Plain Account of Christian Perfection* in order to assert (and reassert) the importance of his belief in entire sanctification, also known as "Christian perfection," throughout his entire ministerial career. In the book, he described entire sanctification the following way:

> [Entire sanctification] is that habitual disposition of soul which, in the sacred writings, is termed holiness; and which directly implies the being cleansed from sin, "from all filthiness both of flesh and spirit;" and, by consequence, the being endued with those virtues which were in Christ Jesus; the being so "renewed in the image of our mind," as to be "perfect as our Father in heaven is perfect."[24]

At the time of conversion, people experience regeneration as well as justification, and regeneration begins the initial sanctification of believers. As God works sanctifying grace, believers have the privilege of benefiting from greater assurance, greater sensitivity to sin, repentance after justification, and desire to be holy—to love God and their neighbors—as Jesus Christ modeled Christian living. The Apostle Paul speaks of this trajectory of spiritual formation in 1 Thessalonians 5:23-24: "May the God of peace himself sanctify you entirely; and may your spirit and soul and body be kept sound and blameless at the coming of our Lord Jesus Christ. The one who calls you is faithful, and he will do this."

One way of thinking about entire sanctification can be illustrated by how Christians refer to Jesus as their Savior and Lord. It is common phraseology; people say: "Jesus is my Savior and Lord!" From Wesley's point of view, people become Christians when they accept Jesus as their Savior. This may occur instantaneously or gradually, in childhood or adulthood; most people's Christian testimony varies, depending upon the particularities of their upbringing, social and religious context, temperament, and so on. But in the life of most Christians, Wesley argued, it is not until sometime subsequent to their conversion that they come to understand that Jesus does not just want to become their Savior but also Lord of their lives.

Of course, Jesus Christ is always Lord, but believers have not always consecrated their lives to his lordship. Jesus' lordship requires a qualitatively different relationship with God, one that is wholly submitted to God in obedience and open to the empowerment of the Holy Spirit. Although people may become entirely sanctified at the time of their conversion, Wesley argued that most do not reach that stage of spiritual maturity, humility, and submission until a later time in their Christian lives. When they reach that "second crisis," as Wesley sometimes called it, and wholly consecrate their lives to God, then God's sanctifying grace works more effectively. Through the presence and power of the Holy Spirit, Christians may experience a quantum leap—so to speak—in their sanctification, when Jesus becomes the Lord of all aspects of their lives and not just their Savior.

To be sure, Wesley was quite hopeful in describing what Christians may expect with regard to holy living once they are entirely sanctified. An example of Wesley's spiritual sanguinity can be found in the introduction to a second volume of hymns, which he quoted in *A Plain Account of Christian Perfection.* I will include only a sample—but still a lengthy sample—of the pastoral verve in Wesley's exhortations for Christians to live holy lives. However, note that Wesley qualifies many of his claims in footnotes, remarking that his past pastoral exhortations needed some proviso, lest people interpret him as promoting a completed perfectionism that he rejected. (In the quotation below, I put the comments from his footnotes in parenthetical brackets.) In description of entirely sanctified Christians, Wesley said:

> They are freed from self-will, as desiring nothing but the holy and perfect will of God; not supplies in want, not ease in pain, [This is far too strong. Our Lord himself desired ease in pain. He asked for it, only with resignation: "Not as I will," I desire, "but as thou wilt."] nor life, or death, or any creature; but continually crying in their inmost soul, "Father, thy will be done." They are freed from evil thoughts, so that they cannot enter into them, no, not for a moment. Aforetime, when an evil thought came in, they looked up, and it vanished away. But now it does not come in, there being no room for this, in a soul which is full of God. They are free from wanderings in prayer. Whensoever they pour out their hearts in a more immediate manner before God, they have no thought of anything past [This is far too strong. See the sermon "On Wandering Thoughts."] or absent, or to come, but of God alone. In times past, they had wandering thoughts darted in, which yet fled away hike smoke; but now that smoke does not rise at all. They have no fear or doubt, either as to their state in general, or

as to any particular action [Frequently this is the case; but only for a time.]. The "unction from the Holy One" teacheth them every hour what they shall do, and what they shall speak [For a time it may be so; but not always.]; nor therefore have they any need to reason concerning it [Sometimes they have no need; at other times they have.]. They are in one sense freed from temptations; for though numberless temptations fly about them, yet they trouble them not [Sometimes they do not; at other times they do, and that grievously.]. At all times their souls are even and calm, their hearts are steadfast and unmovable. Their peace, flowing as a river, "passeth all understanding," and they "rejoice with joy unspeakable and full of glory." For they "are sealed by the Spirit unto the day of redemption," having the witness in themselves, that "there is laid up for" them a "crown of righteousness which the Lord will give" them "in that day" [Not all who are saved from sin; many of them have not attained it yet.].[25]

Wesley's comments above reveal why he is often misinterpreted as advocating a perfectionism that seems impossible biblically as well as experientially. In trying to describe the dynamics of spiritual formation, Wesley tried to hold in tension both his hope and realism with regard to the Christian life. On the one hand, he did not think that Christians should feel defeated about their spiritual prospects. By divine grace, God provides believers with the empowerment to grow spiritually through the means of grace so that they may love God as well as their neighbors, consistently overcoming the trials and temptations experienced in life.

On the other hand, Wesley did not think that Christians were exempt from ongoing challenges spiritually, physically, and socially. While on earth, Christians still experience temptation, sin, evil, pain, and suffering. But they do not need to suffer continuous struggle and defeat; divine help is available. God is present, aiding people through the presence and power of the Holy Spirit, as well as the Bible and the means of grace, to overcome challenges they face. Reflecting upon entire sanctification unquestionably includes theological elements of mystery, as do other theological affirmations. But Wesley believed that God is sufficient to help people live with great hope in overcoming sin and other problems in life, not only for life hereafter, but also here and now.

Was Wesley spiritually unrealistic; overly hopeful? Of course, one can accuse Wesley of anything. Besides, the problems that people experience in life cannot always be easily understood, much less mastered. In fact, there may occur trials and tribulations in life that cannot be mastered, short of a miracle. Be that as it may, Wesley was compelled to make sense, at least, of biblical commands to be perfect, to be holy, to love, and to become more like Jesus Christ. The Bible is full of exhortations to mature, despite the reality of physical, emotional, and social limitations as well as spiritual limitations. Christians need to take those biblical exhortations seriously, according to Wesley, and not consider themselves passive, powerless nonparticipants in the Christian life. Moreover, church history is replete with Christians, from the time of the patristics—both west and east, but especially in the East—who considered holy living a possibility, rather than a principled, albeit inaccessible, goal. That tradition of holy living was carried on in Western Christianity through various saints, mystics, and advocates of spiritual disciplines, such as the Catholic Thomas à Kempis and the Anglican William Law, who both influenced Wesley.

Although Calvin may have advocated obedience through mortification, it was not with the hope of contributing to more victorious Christian living. If growth and maturity occurred, then thanks be to God. But we had nothing directly to contribute to it. By contrast, Wesley said that we can contribute to our spiritual formation, and that we can help to overcome sin, evil, pain, and suffering—all enabled by God's grace. We will never cease facing challenges in our lives, but we are not without means of grace, described in the Bible, by which we may partner with God in overcoming trials, growing spiritually as Christians, and transforming others societally as well as individually.

In describing entire sanctification, Wesley said that Christians will continue to grow. They will never cease learning, maturing, loving, and becoming more like Jesus Christ. Such growth actually increases after entire sanctification, since believers become more sensitive to ongoing sin in their lives and are quicker to try to overcome it by God's grace. The effects of sanctification will affect others socially as well as individually, physically as well as spiritually, and with justice as well as love. Spiritual growth may occur through gradual progress, punctuated by various crisis experiences. But no crisis is as consequential for one's sanctification as the decision—which began, continued, and will be completed by God's grace—to consecrate one's life wholly to Jesus as Lord as well as Savior.

Final Thoughts

Both Wesley and Calvin emphasized sanctification in the lives of Christians. Calvin talked about both the mortification and vivification that occurs in believers. God vivifies people through both justification and sanctification. God continues to work in the lives of believers by mortifying them, lest they forget that they are saved by grace through faith and that they are wholly reliant upon God for all aspects of their salvation. They should mortify their lives as well, since God graciously provided laws in the Bible that help them live more moral and orderly lives.

Wesley also emphasized sanctification, but thought that Christians had far greater reason to hope with regard to the lives to which God calls them here and now. Subsequent to conversion, God's Holy Spirit continues to work in and through the lives of believers. In fact, God provides means of grace in the Bible coupled with the empowerment of the Holy Spirit to help people partner with God in becoming more spiritual; more holy; more loving; more like Jesus Christ. God wants people to engage actively in spiritual disciplines that contribute to their growth, their victory over trials and temptations—always by God's grace. Indeed, Wesley was very hopeful about how Christians may become entirely sanctified. Greater Christlikeness in their lives occurs, not for their sake alone, but for the sake of loving God, and for loving their neighbors in ways that benefit them physically, ethically, and socially as well as spiritually.

Discussion Questions

1. How do you envision the Christian life? Would you argue that, in reality, people ought not to expect too much with regard to over-coming struggles they may experience? Or would you argue that God's grace helps people overcome struggles, rather than being defeated by them?

2. To what extent do Christians need to mortify their lives? What are the benefits of the self-denial of mortification? To what extent should Christians expect that God vivify their lives, enlivening them spiritually?

3. How much responsibility do you believe God gives you in part-nering with the Holy Spirit in partaking of various means of grace (or spiritual disciplines)?

4. What means of grace do you find most helpful in growing spiritu-ally? Prayer? Bible study? The Lord's Supper? Fasting? Christian conference?

5. To what degree do you think that God wants you to become more perfect? More holy? More loving? Is entire sanctification (also known as Christian perfection) a helpful teaching? What are its liabilities?

6. What are ways that you would like to grow more spiritually? What are ways that you believe may help you to grow?

CHURCH: MORE CATHOLIC THAN MAGISTERIAL

And I tell you, you are Peter, and on this rock I will build my church, and the gates of Hades will not prevail against it. (Matthew 16:18)

As a child, I was religiously precocious. That is, I always seemed to have an interest in spiritual matters related to the church. I liked attending church and participating in youth programs, Bible quizzing, summer Christian camps, and other church-related activities. The preaching in church services might not always have been that inspiring, but to me sermons represented only a small slice of church life.

Because of my religious interests and church involvements, I remember people asking me if I was a "PK." The question had to do with whether I was a "preacher's kid." The insinuation insulted me because I was not a preacher's kid; my father was the small-business owner of a plumbing shop. Finally, in frustration, I answered such inquiries with the sarcastic response, "Why yes! I am a PK. How did you know my dad's a plumber?" Usually the sarcasm was lost on them, so I had to drive home the point that people who are religious do not have to be some kind of socially conditioned or reality-challenged person.

As an undergraduate at Stanford University, I decided to major in religious studies. It was not because Stanford was in any way Christian; I received a decidedly secular education in comparative religious studies. But studying all religious traditions, and not just Christianity, fascinated me. As I continued my academic studies in Christian theology, I became aware of biblical, historical, and systematic theology. Although I considered myself to be quite biblical and orthodox in my theology, I still tried to understand and appreciate diverse Christian perspectives.

Over the past two decades, I have become increasingly saddened by the seeming unwillingness of Christians to take the time and effort to try to understand and appreciate the beliefs, values, and practices of others. Part of their unwillingness, in my opinion, has to do with their ignorance. Of course, as I like to say, the root of ignorance is "ignoring," and too many Christians intentionally ignore the beliefs, values, and practices of others, including those of other Christians and churches. This leaves them vulnerable to judgmental and unjust treatment of others different from them. To be sure, I think that some Christians stray too far from biblical and orthodox Christianity. But for the most part, I think that Christians are too quick to judge others negatively, even demonizing them. No wonder non-Christians often view Christians and churches as being very divisive, unloving, and hypocritical in their judgmentalism. What is the cliché? Christians love to set up circular firing squads?

Because of my heightened concern for Christian understanding, cooperation, and unity, I became involved with various ecumenical endeavors—that is, work for unity among Christians and churches. Some dismiss ecumenism as "political correctness," but its origin comes from Jesus' prayer for his disciples to be unified: "I ask not only on behalf of these, but also on behalf of those who will believe in me through their word, that they may all be one. As you, Father, are in me and I am in you, may they also be in us, so that the world may believe that you have sent me" (John 17:20-21).

Wesley and Calvin were very concerned about the nature and mission of the church. We can even say that they gave themselves self-sacrificially for the church. Calvin had to be cautious, since Continental Europeans were still fighting over the Reformation. Even in the city of Geneva, where he experienced governmental protection, personal safety and religious liberty were hazardous. Schism from the Roman Catholic Church had exacerbated turmoil in all dimensions of social, political, and economic life. Along with the other reformers, Calvin had the formidable task of solidifying Protestantism after centuries of Catholic hegemony. Missteps could not only lead to ecclesiastical failure; they could lead to death. Calvin resourcefully responded to the social, political, and economic needs of people as well as their spiritual needs. Thus, Calvin gave leadership to a blend of ecclesiastical and civil authority that helped hold Geneva together, despite various forms of resistance to the Reformation.

Wesley lived in England during the eighteenth century, after the time of the Reformation. But the effects of civil war and religious separatism during the seventeenth century persisted throughout the British Empire; they imperiled those whose beliefs, values, and practices did not coincide with established civil and ecclesiastical authorities. Tension was exacerbated by governmental and church conflict in imperial colonies, for example, in the American colonies, which led to revolution in the eighteenth century—militarily as well as ecclesiastically.

Nature of the Church

Calvin along with Luther contributed much to the doctrine of the church as understood by Protestants. Since both men protested against centuries of church authority and tradition, resourcefulness was required in differentiating Protestantism from Roman Catholicism. Of course, while Luther and Calvin were resourceful, they also considered their understanding of the nature of the church to be faithful to biblical teachings. In addition, they considered themselves faithful to historic creedal affirmations about the church. In the Nicene Creed, for example, the church was described as one, holy, catholic, and apostolic. They agreed that Jesus Christ established one church; however, the true church was more invisible than visibly existent in a single, monolithic institution, such as the Catholic Church. Calvin and Luther agreed that the church is holy, because of the atoning work of Jesus, by which righteousness is imputed to the elect—the true believers. They agreed that the church is catholic, universally embracing the elect regardless of their national, ethnic, linguistic, and other cultural differences. Finally, Calvin and Luther agreed on the apostolic nature of the church. For them, apostolicity had to do with the fidelity of the apostles' preaching and teaching as recorded in the Bible, rather than an unbroken succession of ecclesiastical ordination, as Catholics understood apostolicity.

Calvin's *Institutes* did much to establish Protestant doctrine of the church. He had received an already-established Reformation tradition, founded by leaders such as Luther in Germany, as well as Zwingli, Bucer, and Farel in Switzerland. Although Calvin inherited a rich background of Reformed theology, he did much to consolidate it and advance the influence of Reformed churches.

Calvin wrote about how God instituted the church, with Jesus Christ as the head. According to book IV of the *Institutes,* the church represents the greatest among the various "external means or aids by which God invites us into the society of Christ and holds us therein."[1] Included among these "means or aids" were preaching, teaching, proper administration of the sacraments, and church discipline. Calvin stated a classic Protestant definition of the church: "Wherever we see the Word of God purely preached and heard, and the sacraments administered according to Christ's institution, there, it is not to be doubted, a church of God exists [cf. Eph. 2:20]."[2] Thus, the two distinguishing marks of the church included (1) the pure preaching of the "Word of God" (the Bible), and (2) the proper administration of the sacraments, as Jesus was believed to have instituted them.

Calvin considered the church to be essential to the lives of Christians. Of course, the church is a covenant community, but not solely composed of the elect. Congregants may be baptized, but that does not guarantee that all are elect. Accordingly, infant baptism was not regarded as salvific. Be that as it may, Calvin did regard participation in the church as the typical means of union in Jesus Christ—a union essential to salvation.

Outside the true church—that is, outside the elect—there is no salvation. So abandonment of church affiliation is spiritually "disastrous." Calvin said, "God's fatherly favor and the especial witness of spiritual life are limited to his flock, so that it is always disastrous to leave the church."[3] Of course, since the church is thought to be invisible, more than visible, we cannot be entirely sure about who is elect. Those who attend visible churches may or may not be true believers, yet with the judgment of charity, Calvin thought that all might attend.

Calvin's dedication on behalf of the church is manifestly evident. In his introduction to the *Institutes,* Calvin said, "[S]ince I undertook the office of teacher in the church, I have had no other purpose than to benefit the church."[4] In turn, the church benefits believers. It contributes to their growth through progressive spiritual nurture. Calvin said:

> We see how God, who could in a moment perfect his own, nevertheless desires them to grow up into manhood solely under the education of the church. We see the way set for it: the preaching of the heavenly doctrine has been enjoined upon the pastors. We see that all are brought under the same regulation, that with a gentle and teachable spirit they may allow themselves to be governed by teachers appointed to this function.[5]

Through gentleness, teachability, and obedience, Christians live as they ought. Their outward actions are not intended to contribute to their sanctification; increase of sanctification remains in the spiritual purview of God. As Calvin said, "For, although God's power is not bound to outward means, he has nonetheless bound us to this ordinary manner of teaching. Fanatical men, refusing to hold fast to it, entangle themselves in many deadly snares."[6] Fanaticism, according to Calvin, referred to those with a theologically false view of the church, which included Anabaptists as well as Roman Catholics.

In defining the true church, Calvin also determined false churches. With regard to compliance with the aforementioned marks of the church (namely, proclamation of the word and proper administration of the sacraments), the Roman Catholic Church failed. It represented the "tyranny of Antichrist," which Calvin discussed with eschatological seriousness.[7] In particular, he accused the popes of being "Antichrists."[8] Catholic preaching was not thought to represent pure biblical teaching, and Calvin argued that its sacramentalism distorted the nature of practices instituted by Jesus Christ. To these doctrinal failures, others were added that warranted the "protests" of the reformers, which resulted in the schism between Protestants and Catholics. Of course, the epitome of church abuse was thought to occur through the ecclesiastical and jurisdictional misuse of power, especially by the papacy. Calvin accused popes—both past and present—of abusing civil as well as church authority, oppressing the freedom of believers, corrupting the purity of church doctrine, and treating all people with savage tyranny and butchery.[9] Although Calvin argued for the need for unity among Christians, schism from the Catholic Church as a whole was thought to be biblically and morally justified, despite the presence of a few faithful Catholic churches that met the test of the true marks of a church.

Calvin was heavily invested in polemics—that is, defense of the orthodoxy of Protestantism, especially that of the Reformed tradition's understanding of biblical Christianity. He thought some doctrinal consensus could be achieved among the foremost Protestant reformers. For example, Calvin signed a modified version of the Lutheran Augsburg Confession, revised by Melanchthon, entitled the *Variata*. Accordingly, "if the true church is the pillar and foundation of truth [I Tim. 3:15]," then the church must defend its beliefs, values, and practices from others, especially so-called churches that, because of ignorance or tyranny, promote heresy and deserve censure, excommunication, and discipline. According to Calvin, Catholics certainly deserved the discipline of the church, as did Anabaptists and others—individually and collectively—who stood against the reformers, in general, and Reformed theology, in particular. Against such antagonists, Calvin was highly polemical and condemnatory.

Magisterial Church

Sometimes Calvin's view of the church is referred to as "magisterial." This reference is, in part, because of his prominence along with that of Luther and other founding reformers who gave authoritative leadership to the Protestant Reformation. As such, their leadership is sometimes referred to as the "magisterial Reformation," reminiscent at least of the teaching authority of the Roman Catholic magisterium.

Another meaning of *magisterial* has to do with the collaboration Calvin articulated and promoted between the church and state—between ecclesiastical and civil governance. Some followers of Calvin consider this collaboration to have been archaic, a mistake "of his age," for which Calvin and the Reformation should not be held accountable.[10] After all, did Calvin not stand up against the authoritarian governance of the Roman Catholic Church, protesting its tyranny of papal imperiousness? Was he not a kinder and gentler leader than the Catholics?

It is a matter of debate, even among the followers of Calvin, with regard to his precise understanding of the relationship between church and state. Some argue that Calvin promoted a closer relationship between ecclesiastical and civil governance during the earlier years of his leadership role in Geneva but that he later demarcated a clearer separation between church and state. In his last edition of the *Institutes,* for example, Calvin most clearly separated the church's power to excommunicate from the state's power to coerce and use violence, but he still argued that the state should implement discipline on behalf of the church.[11] As such, Calvin continued to approve of the right and responsibility of civil magistrates—or deputies, vicars, and other rulers—to banish, punish, and even execute people on behalf of church censures and excommunications.[12]

How ardently Calvin argued for this collaboration between church and state will, no doubt, remain a matter of debate. But that he believed in and utilized such collaboration is historically undeniable. Moreover, those who followed Calvin's teachings utilized similar civil, political, economic, and other coercive means in order to implement church beliefs, values, and practices. Evidence for such magisterial authority and power can easily be found in Reformed confessions written in the century following his life.

During Calvin's time of ecclesiastical leadership in Geneva, he participated in a *consistoire* (or council). The council served as a church court consisting of pastors, teachers, and ruling elders. It had responsibility for judging the theological and ethical activities of the Genevan citizenry, meting out ecclesiastical judgments and discipline. Initially, the court had power over the life and death of Genevan citizens. However, in time, the civil government alone retained the authority to banish, punish, and execute people. Still, the magistrates of Geneva implemented judgments and discipline determined by the council.

Calvin's magisterial approach to leadership had benefits as well as liabilities. On the one hand, Calvin represented one of the premiere reformers along with Luther, Zwingli, Farel, and Melanchthon. He thus deserved the right to make authoritative pronouncements about what it meant to be Protestant, and to advance those pronouncements with passion and forcefulness, if needed. On the other hand, Calvin's magisterial leadership included authoritarian governance, which intermingled church and civil authority. From Calvin's perspective, God instituted two governments, which is similar to what Luther believed. First, there is the spiritual and eternal government, and the church is mostly concerned about this authority. Second, there is also the civil and earthly government, and magistrates have moral as well as juridical authority over Christian life and society. In Book IV of the *Institutes,* see Calvin's chapters "4. The magistracy is ordained by God," "7. The coercive character of magistracy does not hinder its recognition," and "10. The magistrates' exercise of force is compatible with piety."[13]

Followers of Calvin, who emphasize greater separation between the church and state, consider Calvin's view of the collaboration between ecclesiastical and civil governance to have been a reflection of his historical context, rather than a permanent biblical teaching. The argument is that, if Calvin lived today, then he would not have intermingled the two governances—that is, at least not as he did in the sixteenth century. However, everyone is situated in a particular time and place. We cannot praise Calvin for being ahead of his time, so to speak, in some of his theological reforms, and excuse him for being a product of his time with regard to other ecclesiastical and civil issues. After all, Calvin's rejection of the separation of church and state had far-reaching implications for his own time as well as for those who followed him in the Reformed tradition.

Calvin set a theological precedent that some have described as theocratic—that is, government led by political leaders who are thought to be God's appointed representatives (or magistrates) in ecclesiastical as well as civic governance, guided by God, and with authority to use government to regulate the church as well as society. Now, people may consider the term theocratic off-putting, but Calvin certainly considered Christian involvement in politics as legitimate and important. To be sure, the church and state had different purviews and tasks, but their relationship was complementary rather than separate. Consequently, church leaders such as Calvin were expected to give input in civil matters alongside magistrates in governing society.

Calvin's precise relationship with the civil government in Geneva was complicated. He was a French émigré who initially qualified only for the lowest status of citizenship in the city. Over time, Calvin reached a higher level of citizenship, which allowed him greater status and civil service, though he remained subject to both ecclesiastical and civil supervision. He did not directly have authority to dispense ecclesiastical, civil, and disciplinary judgments. But Calvin still believed that the state—rather than the pope or the king—had the divine right to rule over society. And he actively supported the Genevan magistrates' right to do so. Now, one can argue, that theocracy is good when the leaders are good, godly people, and Calvin would have uplifted Geneva as an example. Of course, bad, ungodly people may also lead theocracies. Such was Calvin's argument, in part, against the tyranny of the Roman Catholic Church and its relationship with the Holy Roman Empire.

In Geneva, Calvin held that magistrates had the right to enforce ecclesiastical laws, decided upon by the council. Such discipline, according to Calvin, was essential to the life of the church. He said, "[I]f no society, indeed, no house which has even a small family, can be kept in proper condition without discipline, it is much more necessary in the church, whose condition should be as ordered as possible."[14] Among the chief uses of church discipline were theological censures and excommunication, or at least their threat of usage. Calvin thought that discipline needed to be strong within society as a whole, as well as in churches. Of course, these beliefs were not new to Calvin. Throughout church history, Christians have repeatedly intermingled ecclesiastical and civil governance. Such beliefs were considered to be tried and true as well as biblical. Consequently, in order to make ecclesiastical laws compulsory, civil law and governance needed to enforce church discipline. And magistrates were responsible for punishing offenders of ecclesiastical laws as well as for other governmental tasks, such as administering taxes and engaging in the military protection of society.

Usually civil enforcement of ecclesiastical laws was mundane, having to do with oversight of the daily actions of people. In Geneva, church attendance was mandatory, and failure to attend resulted in the payment of fines. The government appointed authorities to watch over the morals of people, for example, with regard to clothing worn and speech used as well as more brazen acts of adultery and blasphemy. The latter indiscretions were punishable by censure, fine, excommunication, banishment, and even death. Witchcraft along with incorrigible adultery and heresy were leading reasons for capital punishment by beheading or burning at the stake.

Without doubt, Calvin received the most criticism in Geneva for his endorsement of the harshest church and civil punishment: death. Now, given his context, the execution of people for their religious beliefs and practices predated Calvin. For example, Zwingli, who was the leading Swiss reformer prior to Calvin, persecuted Anabaptists, among others. Keep in mind, though, that ecclesiastical differences sometimes had political, economic, and military implications. For example, military drafts were often dependent upon people's citizenship being certified by infant baptisms. When Anabaptists rejected infant baptism, there occurred political, economic, and military complications as well as ecclesiastical disagreement.

Crimes against church and state invoked capital punishment that included drowning, beheading, or burning at the stake. Calvin supported these punishments, and consented to hundreds of banishments and executions, based upon purported moral dereliction or heresy.[15] There is disagreement among historians, however, with regard to the degree and severity with which theological heresy was punished, at least with regard to its severest form.[16] In fact, some argue that only one person was executed for heresy—Michael Servetus. But most historians think that other punishments, including capital punishment, occurred because of people's theological challenge to the Genevan powers that be.

The most infamous execution (or martyrdom, depending on one's perspective) was that of Servetus, a Spaniard. Servetus was thought to hold heretical views, disputing against the Trinity and infant baptism. Even though he was not a citizen of Geneva, Servetus visited the city and was arrested, convicted of heresy by the council, and burned at the stake. Calvin wrote a theological pamphlet condemning Servetus, though he requested a less severe method of execution than burning at the stake; but he condoned the execution nonetheless.[17] In a 1561 letter to Monseigneur du Poet, chamberlain to the king of Navarre, Calvin reasserted the need to suppress theological disagreement, uplifting the execution of Servetus as a model. He said:

> Above all, do not fail to rid the country of all those zealous scoundrels that stir up the people by their discourses to make head against us, blacken our conduct, and wish to make our belief pass for a reverie. Such monsters should be smothered, as I have done here, by the execution of Michel Servetus the Spaniard. Do not imagine that in future any one will take it into his head to do the like.[18]

The "scoundrels" to whom Calvin alluded included Roman Catholics, Anabaptists, and other Christians who held beliefs thought to be in conflict with biblical Christianity. Calvin's polemical zeal became so well known that some of his Reformation compatriots were appalled by his heavy-handed use of civil authority to execute those judged to be apostate. Luther, for example, said of Calvin's actions in Geneva: "With a death sentence they solve all argumentation."[19]

Although one may argue that Calvin was overly influenced by the coercive and violent era in which he lived, similar practices did not soon subside after him. Followers of Calvin continued to appeal to the collaboration between church and civil authority. The Belgic Confession (1618), for example, elevated discipline as a third Protestant mark of the church, and the

Westminster Confession (1646) affirmed the following with regard to the authority "of the civil magistrate":

> The civil magistrate may not assume to himself the administration of the word and sacraments, or the power of the keys of the kingdom of heaven; yet he hath authority, and it is his duty, to take order, that unity and peace be preserved in the church, that the truth of God be kept pure and entire, that all blasphemies and heresies be suppressed, all corruptions and abuses in worship and discipline prevented or reformed, and all the ordinances of God duly settled, administrated, and observed.[20]

Calvin provided the precedent of a magisterial-oriented church, which relied upon civil as well as ecclesiastical collaboration for the enforcement of discipline. Indeed, it included harsh suppression of theological differences in addition to punishing ethical transgressions.

To be sure, it can be argued that "there is a season, and a time for every matter" (Ecclesiastes 3:1), and Calvin's strength of mission was what made him successful, along with other reformers, in finally overturning the domination of the Roman Catholic Church and, to a certain extent, the Holy Roman Empire. Without liberative protestation, apologetics, and polemics, would reformers like Luther and Calvin have been successful in the establishment of Protestantism in the sixteenth century without hard-nosed protestation, apologetics, and polemics? Does to think otherwise sound like naive armchair commentary upon the heroic leadership of reformers who staked their lives upon their most cherished beliefs and values?

Today, Christians may no longer execute literal religious executions. But Calvin's magisterial approach toward those who disagree with Reformed theology may result in more than mere disapproval. Basically, Calvin advocated use of any political, economic, or cultural power available for guarding Christianity as well as for advancing Christian beliefs, values, and practices in society and in the church. It is the responsibility of Christians, according to Calvin, to maintain the biblical purity of the church and to use disciplinary means available to enforce similar purity in society—ecclesiastically and civilly; polemically and politically; coercively and juridically.

Calvin may have granted a measure of acceptance toward those with whom he mostly agreed and shared leadership in the Reformation, such as Luther and Melanchthon. But he exhibited scant tolerance and forbearance toward those who disagreed with him and who were not people of social, political, or ecclesiastical stature. Calvin's magisterial approach to collaborating ecclesiastical authority and power with civil authority and power—with all its political, economic, and cultural might—was a model his followers used repeatedly. They may not have resorted to capital punishment, but his followers believed that it was theologically right and good to use persuasive and coercive means to suppress both the church and state in advancing the Reformed understanding of biblical Christianity.

Faithful Beliefs, Faithful Living

Wesley agreed with much of what Calvin had to say about the nature of the church. In his sermon entitled "Of the Church," Wesley affirmed the wording of the Anglican Thirty-Nine Articles (1563), which was a variation of the Augsburg Confession. Wesley said:

> This account is exactly agreeable to the nineteenth Article of our Church, the Church of England—only the Article includes a little more than the Apostle has expressed.

> *Of the Church*
> *The visible church of Christ is a congregation of faithful men, in which the pure word of God is preached, and the sacraments be duly administered.*

> It may be observed that at the same time our Thirty-nine Articles were compiled and published a Latin translation of them was published by the same authority. In this the words were *coetus credentium,* "a congregation of believers," plainly showing that by "faithful men" the compilers meant men endued with "living faith." This brings the Article to a still nearer agreement to the account given by the Apostle.[21]

Just as Calvin read the original Augsburg Confession and requested a qualification, which Melanchthon provided in the *Variata,* Wesley qualified his description of the church. Throughout his life and ministry, Wesley emphasized that the church ought to be more than a congregation of believers—more than "faithful men"; it ought to also exhibit "living faith." It is not enough for people to exhibit right belief (or *orthodoxy*); they ought to also exhibit a right heart (*orthokardia*) and right practice (*orthopraxis*). From Wesley's perspective, the devil (as well as other religious people) may hold to "orthodoxy or right opinions," but "may all the while be as great a stranger as he to religion of the heart."[22] Both faithful people and faithful living were constitutive of the church—of true believers. Salvation included God's election, rightly understood from the perspective of prevenient grace, but it also included love for God and neighbor, which is a more relational than doctrinal understanding of Christianity.

Wesley had a less dogmatic and polemical approach in understanding the doctrines of the church than did Calvin. From Wesley's perspective, no one could reasonably be expected to agree on every doctrine and theological issue. To expect uniformity ran the risk of expulsing almost every Christian outside one's particular understanding of the church. Certainly one cannot be indifferent to religious teachings contrary to the Bible and to historic Christianity, and Wesley did his fair share of polemicism. However, not everyone interprets the Bible the same way, and not every development in doctrine, worship, and congregational life was understood the same way in church history. Greater flexibility rather than rigidity was needed in relations among Christians, churches, and emerging denominations. Thus, with regard to defining the church, Wesley said:

> I will not undertake to defend the accuracy of this definition. I dare not exclude from the church catholic all those congregations in which any unscriptural doctrines which cannot be affirmed to be "the pure Word of God" are sometimes, yea, frequently preached. Neither all those congregations in which the sacraments are not "duly 'administered." Certainly if these things are so the Church of Rome is not so much as a part of the catholic church; seeing therein neither is "the pure Word of God" preached nor the sacraments "duly administered." Whoever they are that have "one Spirit, one hope, one lord, one faith, one God and Father of all," I can easily bear with their holding wrong opinions, yea, and superstitious models of worship. Nor would I on these accounts scruple still to include them within the pale of the catholic church. Neither would I have any objection to receive them, if they desired it, as members of the Church of England.[23]

Wesley was loyal to the Church of England throughout his life. He wanted to maintain unity, of some sort, rather than minister at odds with other Christians. To be sure, there existed tensions in his relationship with Anglican leaders, but he worked through those tensions rather than giving up on the prospect of continued membership in the Church of England. In the fledgling United States, the formation of the Methodist Episcopal Church had been far more the result of necessity than of any grand scheme. Withdrawal of Anglican priests from North America during the Revolutionary War left few options for dealing with the ongoing spiritual and church needs of people.

Wesley was irenic—that is, he sought ways in which to collaborate with other Christians, especially for the sake of unity in ministry. His irenicism extended to Roman Catholics as well as to Protestant nonconformists such as the Anabaptists, Society of Friends (Quakers), and nascent Pentecostals. Anglicans had, after all, broken away from Catholicism, just as had Calvin and other Continental reformers. And there remained tensions between Protestants and Catholics even in Britain. But Wesley did not consider fellowship and the possibility of cooperation with Catholics to be improper. On the contrary, in his open "Letter to a Roman Catholic," Wesley said:

> O brethren, let us not still fall out by the way! I hope to see you in heaven. And if I practise the religion above described, you dare not say I shall go to hell. You cannot think so. None can persuade you to it. Your own conscience tells you the contrary. Then if we cannot as yet think alike in all things, at least we may love alike. Herein we cannot possibly do amiss. For of one point none can doubt a moment,—"God is love; and he that dwelleth in love, dwelleth in God, and God in him."[24]

The words of Wesley are quite irenic, quite ecumenical, considering the fact that he still lived during a time of political and military conflicts between Protestants and Catholics. Wesley's openness to fellowship with, and cooperation alongside, other Christian traditions represented an ecumenical spirit far ahead of his time in the history of the church.

Catholic Spirit

Wesley's irenic and ecumenical spirit is often referred to as his "catholic spirit," which was the title of one of his early sermons. Remember that the Nicene Creed referred to the church as "catholic," which expressed how God universally embraces all people into fellowship regardless of their national, ethnic, linguistic, and other cultural differences. Among these differences, Wesley included differences of doctrinal or theological opinion. But this does not mean that he was indifferent to the Bible or to orthodox Christian doctrine. On the contrary, Wesley was very aware of them. He did not think, however, that the church should be defined primarily by its doctrines and disapproval expressed toward others as much as by its irenicism and love expressed toward them, both inside and outside the church.

In his sermon "Catholic Spirit," Wesley carefully explained what he did not mean by a catholic spirit. For example, it did not include indifference to all opinions or theological viewpoints. Wesley said, "A catholic spirit is not speculative latitudinarianism," which promoted religious pluralism; "A catholic spirit is not any kind of practical latitudinarianism," which allowed unrestricted, disorderly worship practices in church; and "A catholic spirit is not indifference to all congregations," which made no distinctions whatsoever between emerging as well as already existing denominations.[25] Such differences needed to be studied, discussed, and assessed based upon the best of what can be known through the Bible, church tradition, critical thinking, and relevant experience.

To Wesley, it was important that Christians be of a right heart. He often spoke of "heart-religion," and thought it best described a love-centered understanding of Christianity and the church. After all, a "catholic spirit" actually means a "catholic love." In the conclusion to his sermon, Wesley said:

> If, then, we take this word in the strictest sense, a man of a catholic spirit is one who, in the manner above-mentioned, gives his hand to all whose hearts are right with his heart: one who knows how to value, and praise God for, all the advantages he enjoys, with regard to the knowledge of the things of God, the true scriptural manner of worshipping him, and, above all, his union with a congregation fearing God and working righteousness: one who, retaining these blessings with the strictest care, keeping them as the apple of his eye, at the same time loves—as friends, as brethren in the Lord, as members of Christ and children of God, as joint partakers now of the present kingdom of God, and fellow heirs of his eternal kingdom—all, of whatever opinion or worship, or congregation, who believe in the Lord Jesus Christ; who love God and man; who, rejoicing to please, and fearing to offend God, are careful to abstain from evil, and zealous of good works. [26]

Does this mean that there is no need for discipline within the church? On the contrary, Wesley firmly believed in its importance. He was no advocate for latitudinarianism, which was the eighteenth-century way of talking about religious pluralism. In his sermon "Causes of the Inefficacy of Christianity," Wesley said, "Now, wherever doctrine is preached, where there is not discipline, it cannot have its full effect upon the hearers."[27] So he certainly was not indifferent either to doctrine or church discipline, but the discipline came through the church and accountability among Christians. This discipline included censure and the expulsion of individuals and groups of individuals, but it did not use juridical and punitive functions of civil government. Nor did Wesley resort to other political, economic, and institutional means to coerce compliance in religious matters.

Wesley spoke in his writings about differences between Calvin and himself, and between Calvinists and Methodists. But perhaps one of the most telling differences between them occurred with regard to the relationship between the church and civil government. Wesley was appreciative of civil government, and, relatively speaking, was quite conservative in his homage to the monarchy of Britain. However, Wesley strongly disagreed with the civil, political, and other coercive elements of Calvin's Reformed tradition. In his "Dialogue between a Predestinarian and His Friend," Wesley said: "I think it cannot be found in holy writ, and that it is a plant which bears dismal fruit. An instance of which we have in Calvin himself; who confesses that he procured the burning to death of Michael Servetus, purely for differing from him in opinion in matters of religion."[28] Wesley was aware of the fatal implications of Calvin's theological disciplinarianism, and he was not just speaking figuratively with regard to violence toward others, done on behalf of the Reformed tradition. Wesley countered such authoritarianism by emphasizing the need for a more catholic—rather than magisterial—approach to understanding the church and its mission in the world.

Final Thoughts

Both Wesley and Calvin dedicated their lives to the church—to its establishment and to its flourishing theologically, spiritually, and ministerially. Their efforts were successful, and their influence spread far beyond Geneva and Britain. It is undeniable that Calvin's church influence spread throughout the world, aiding many Christians, and not just those within the Reformed tradition. Likewise, Methodism became a worldwide contributor to ministering on behalf of the gospel of Jesus Christ.

But Wesley and Calvin differed, at least in two ways. First, Wesley thought that there should be far more flexibility among Christians and churches with regard to the degree to which they agreed or disagreed about doctrinal and ecclesiastical issues. Calvin was far more polemical, emphasizing the need to engage constantly in apologetics and to purify the church through censure, excommunication, and whatever suppressive means could be meted out. To be sure, Calvin and Wesley lived in different sociocultural times. However, the times were not so different that a greater degree of irenicism and ecumenism would not earlier have been beneficial. Without sacrificing essential biblical beliefs, values, and practices, Wesley believed that love and not dogmatism should characterize the nature of the church.

Second, Wesley did not think that the civil government should be involved with the juridical and punitive responsibilities of the church. He was not unaware of the complications of the relationship between church and state. After all, he lived in Britain wherein the Church of England was the state church. However, he disagreed with Calvin's union of church and civil authority. The civil authority of the state should provide religious freedom, rather than restrict or prohibit it. Wesley and Britain were well aware of the religious motives that had fueled violence and civil war against individual Christians and churches in the preceding century. To be sure, Wesley had not achieved the level of ecclesiastical and civil authority that Calvin achieved in Geneva. But he did not see the virtue of uniting church and state, as had Calvin; church and state may have existed in complementary ways, but a collaboration of the two was not rightly reflective of biblical teaching. The reign of God in the world had far more to do with the church than with the government. Nor were collaborative entanglements between the church and state wise, given the experience of Christians in church in history. After all, Wesley knew that the alliance between church and state could become unholy, resulting in deplorable methods of unjust persecution for differences in religious opinion that neither the Bible nor civility sanctioned.

Discussion Questions

1. Does a gathering of Christians constitute a church? In what sense does the church consist of Christians, collectively speaking, and in what sense does it consist of a place, rather than individuals?

2. What would you describe as the distinguishing marks of the church? Are they one, holy, catholic, and apostolic? Are they the preaching of the pure word of God (the Bible), and the proper administration of the sacraments? Both?

3. What is the relationship between the church and civil government? How actively should civil governments be involved in churches? Contrariwise, how actively should Christians and churches be involved in civil government?

4. What is the role of church discipline? How important is it for the life of the church and its members? How ought church discipline occur?

5. How polemical and apologetical should churches be, and how irenic and ecumenical should they be?

6. Given the fact that not all Christians and churches agree with all matters of faith and practice, how should they relate with one another? How might they cooperate with one another, for example, in ministry?

Chapter 8

MINISTRY: MORE EMPOWERING THAN TRIUMPHAL

Therefore, since it is by God's mercy that we are engaged in this ministry, we do not lose heart. (2 Corinthians 4:1)

When I began formal ministry, I served as an assistant pastor of a church located in a small farming community in the San Joaquin valley of California. My primary pastoral responsibilities had to do with youth work and small group ministries. I particularly enjoyed working with small groups, since they played an important role in my nurture as a Christian. During the time I was in high school, I was encouraged by family and friends to participate regularly in a small group of Christians. Together we studied the Bible, prayed, participated in various ministries, and held one another accountable spiritually and in other ways.

Over the years, I participated in small groups in college, seminary, and graduate school. While undergoing seminary and theological training, I became more aware of Wesley's vast development of small group ministries. He developed Methodist societies of men and women who met midweek in order to supplement Sunday worship in Anglican churches; he developed class meetings that consisted of approximately a dozen Christians who could provide more accountability; and he developed bands (or select societies) of same-gender participants who desired more rigorous accountability for the promotion of holy living. Wesley wrote questions that could be regularly asked in order to provoke and empower participants to grow spiritually and to minister to others, individually and collectively.

In my experience, it seemed that the more accountable I became with others in a small group, the more effective it was in helping me to nurture as a Christian. I grew spiritually, intellectually, emotionally, and relationally. I also grew in terms of how I ministered and in how I envisioned ministry. The more I interacted with other Christians in small groups, the more I learned about the variety of ways there are to love others in tangible, physical, and just ways as well as in spiritual ways, with which I was more familiar.

Small group contexts have been for me the place in which I experienced the greatest growth and empowerment as a Christian. Sunday worship experiences have also been important in my spiritual development, just as have other church programs. But the vitality and vision for Christian life and ministry came more from small groups and one-on-one interaction that I had with fellow Christians.

Wesley and Calvin were both very involved with ministries in the church. They self-sacrificially worked individually and collectively for the sake of building up Christians as well as for the glory of God. Of course, their approaches to ministry differed, despite numerous similarities. Those differences were significant, though, and it is important to understand their respective priorities and practices.

Calvin's approach to ministry was more formal, "top-down," and authoritarian in orientation. He promoted a rather conventional approach to ministry, basing it upon the Bible, with emphasis upon church work being done "decently and in order" (1 Corinthians 14:40). Christians ministered primarily through proclamation of the word—the Bible—and proper administration of the sacraments, which celebrated the triumph of God's sovereignty and grace. For Wesley, ministry was not limited to those ministries explicitly described in the Bible. Ministry needed to be creative and responsive to the needs of people and society, led by the presence and work of the Holy Spirit, who continues to lead and empower churches as well as individuals. As a result, Wesley was more innovative than was Calvin in ministering to people's many needs, especially empowering the laity in ministerial leadership.

Varieties of Ministry

Before I investigate the ministries of Wesley and Calvin, let me begin by talking about the varieties of ministry in church history. All approaches to ministry claim to reflect God's mission—God's work in the world. To be sure, it is God and not us who graciously brings about genuine spiritual increase to our lives and ministries. Yet, Christians seek to follow obediently God's call upon their lives, individually and collectively, to participate with God in ministry to the world. The Bible, in particular, represents the fountainhead for conceiving and implementing Christian ministry as the Holy Spirit leads and guides in implementing God's mission.

Although Christians look to the Bible in formulating their ministry, a variety of ministries developed in church history. At the expense of making rather broad generalizations about ministry, several approaches to it are identifiable. For example, some ministries may be described as evangelical, sacramental, contemplative, studious, holiness, activist, charismatic, ecumenical, and so on. Of course, most approaches to ministry cannot be characterized by simply one of the aforementioned categories of ministry. Two or more of the categories may apply to a particular church or denomination, or one category may predominate while others represent secondary or tertiary emphases. Ideally, one could argue that all of the aforementioned categories should apply, at least to church ministries. Even the Apostle Paul talks about the church as a body with "many members, and all the members of the body, though many, are one body" (1 Corinthians 12:12; cf. 12:12-31). This analogy is often applied to local churches, but it also applies to the worldwide church. With such an understanding, different churches (and denominations) may undertake ministry in ways that complement—rather than contradict—the ministries of other churches.

Together the varieties of ministry contribute to an overall unity that is stronger than what individual churches (and denominations) can accomplish. Correspondingly, the diverse ministries contribute to the whole of ministry worldwide. Thus, in comparing the ministries of Wesley and Calvin, I do not say that one is right and one is wrong. Nor do Wesley and Calvin represent all of the aforementioned traditions of ministry. Still, how they ministered and what they said about ministry powerfully influenced those who followed their lead. As the Apostle Paul also said, "On the contrary, the members of the body that seem to be weaker are indispensable, and those members of the body that we think less honorable we clothe with greater honor, and our less respectable members are treated with greater respect" (1 Corinthians 12:22-23).

Just as there are varieties of ministry, there are also varieties of leadership styles. This variety can be found in the Bible as well as in church history. So I do not say that one particular approach to ministry or ministry leadership is needful, and that others are needless. Such a view is neither biblical nor reasonable. Throughout this book, I have tried to say that Calvin is a theological giant in church history, and his leadership and theological contributions to ministry should not be minimized. However, despite his excellences, Calvin is not the sole role model for Christians, including Protestant Christians. Moreover, not everyone who considers Calvin to be a ministerial or leadership role model actually follows him. In such instances, I argue that Wesley represents a more compelling role model that many Christians follow without actually realizing it, which is a thesis for which I have argued throughout this book.

Calvin's View of Ministry

Calvin had a formal, established understanding of ministry, clearly presented in the *Institutes*. From his perspective, the ministry of the church primarily involved proclamation of the gospel and proper administration of the sacraments. Calvin talked about "Word and sacrament," and that phrase is frequently used to describe Calvin's view of ministry—to proclaim God's "Word" and to administer properly baptism and the "Sacred Supper" or "Lord's Supper."[1]

Undoubtedly, one of the greatest strengths of Calvin's understanding of ministry was preaching. In his own life and ministry, he preached thousands of times, especially while he ministered in Geneva. It is unclear whether Calvin was ordained in a customary way. Biographer John McNeill believes that Calvin was ordained, though he admits that the details of Calvin's ordination are somewhat uncertain.[2] Be that as it may, Calvin's primary ministry occurred through his preaching, teaching, writing, and spreading of Reformed theology. Of course, he believed that Reformed theology encapsulated biblical, Christian theology; Calvin did not intend to be sectarian, but to restore churches to historic orthodoxy. As such, he bequeathed a remarkable Christian tradition of excellence in biblical preaching, and Protestants have benefited tremendously from his legacy of proclaiming the gospel.

Calvin's emphasis on the sacraments included the two sacraments of baptism and the Lord's Supper, which resembled Luther and most other reformers. These sacraments were understood differently from the Roman Catholic Church both in quantity and quality. Similar to Luther, though with slight differences, Calvin emphasized how the "Word"—the Bible—clarifies how God offers, guarantees, and seals the promise of divine forgiveness through the sign made by the visible elements of the sacraments: water, bread, and wine. Calvin affirmed infant baptism, which "best accords with Christ's institution and the nature of the sign."[3] Furthermore, Calvin affirmed the Lord's Supper and how "union with Christ" is its "special fruit."[4]

In addition to these ministries, Calvin was involved in a variety of other church practices. After all, he had to help the fledgling Protestants of the Reformed tradition develop church practices that were no longer drawn from Roman Catholicism. For example, Calvin worked to develop liturgical and sacramental practices that included a psalter, catechism, and liturgies for baptism and the Lord's Supper. He wrote prayers for public use as well as

107

prayers for all his sermons. Finally, Calvin wrote guides for pious living on Christian life, ethics, and pastoral care, such as counseling those in crisis and visiting the sick and dying.

Although Calvin did not regard discipline a mark of the church, as discussed in the previous chapter, discipline still represented an important part of ministry. Discipline did not become a mark of the church until later church developments among Calvinists, but its prominence in the Reformed tradition is undeniable. So, if discipline is important for ministry, then extensive pastoral attention must be paid toward pastors holding church members accountable for their beliefs, values, and practices. Likewise, extensive homiletic attention must be paid toward polemics against those who fall short of the Reformed understanding of the Bible, and punishing as well as chastising those who think, speak, and act contrary to it.

During Calvin's ministry in Geneva, great amounts of attention, time, and governance were applied toward securing the triumph, so to speak, of Reformed theology in the Swiss city and beyond, especially in his beloved home country of France. Calvin appointed pastors to go to France in order to spread teachings of the *Institutes* throughout French-speaking lands, and Reformed theology indeed spread throughout Europe. He contributed much to the sustainability of the Reformation, vis-à-vis the Roman Catholic Church, providing strength in Protestant apologetics as well as polemics. It is a tribute to Calvin's leadership and the excellence of his Christian scholarship, especially as found in the *Institutes,* that his Reformed interpretation of orthodox, Christian theology prevailed over many other Protestant teachings as well as those of Catholicism.

Leadership in Ministry

In establishing leadership in ministry, Calvin appealed to the teachings of Ephesians 4:11: "The gifts he gave were that some would be apostles, some prophets, some evangelists, some pastors and teachers." Although the context of the passage deals with divine "gifts," Calvin also speaks of them as "offices." Five offices are mentioned: apostles, prophets, evangelists, pastors, and teachers. However, Calvin considered the first three offices to be limited mostly to the first century. Only the offices of pastor and teacher—two offices inextricably bound up with each other—were considered operative for permanent ministry within the church. Calvin said: "[I]n order that the preaching of the gospel might flourish, he deposited this treasure in the church. He instituted 'pastors and teachers' (Eph. 4:11) through whose lips he might teach his own; he furnished them with authority; finally, he omitted nothing that might make for holy agreement of faith and for right order."[5] Christian preaching and teaching were very important to Calvin both for right faith and right order. Ecclesiastical orderliness as well as right beliefs helped pastors and teachers to sustain the correctness of church and ministry. Accurate instruction in the Bible was especially important for the sustainability of the church and for its ministry. Calvin said:

> We see how God, who could in a moment perfect his own, nevertheless desires them to grow up into manhood solely under the education of the church. We see the way set for it: the preaching of the heavenly doctrine has been enjoined upon the pastors. We see that all are brought under the same regulation, that with a gentle and teachable spirit they may allow themselves to be governed by teachers appointed to this function.[6]

Calvin believed that the ministry represented a function of God's providence. Just as God is sovereign over all of creation, God is sovereign over the church and ministry. And God appointed pastors and teachers to serve in leadership. So believers are dependent upon the high office of pastoral and teaching ministries for their spiritual direction and nurture. In a sense, pastors and teachers were thought to embody the guardians of the church's ministries. Of course, the efficacy of the church and its ministries is reliant upon God's grace, rather than upon human contributions to them. Since it is God alone who is ultimately responsible for the fruit of the church's ministries, we may rest assured despite either increases or decreases in the size and effectiveness of the church. In every circumstance, God is to be praised, since God has sovereign control over all.

Calvin considered the offices of apostle, prophet, and evangelist, mentioned in Ephesians 4:11, to be temporary offices because they primarily existed to establish the church in the first century. As such, their ministerial functions could be described as "lower in rank."[7] Their ministries were exceptional and generally unrepeatable, especially because of the final compilation of the Bible. With regard to the offices of apostle, prophet, and evangelist, Calvin said:

> According to this interpretation (which seems to me to be in agreement with both the words and opinion of Paul), these three functions were not established in the church as permanent ones, but only for that time during which churches were to be erected where none existed before, or where they were to be carried over from Moses to Christ. Still, I do not deny that the Lord has sometimes at a later period raised up apostles, or at least evangelists in their place, as has happened in our own day. For there was need for such persons to lead the church back from the rebellion of Antichrist. Nonetheless, I call this office "extraordinary," because in duly constituted churches it has no place.[8]

109

According to Calvin, the offices of apostle, prophet, and evangelist were "extraordinary" or temporary ministerial functions. They ceased to exist after the first century, or are rare, at best. John McNeill, who edited the *Institutes,* notes that Calvin thought that Luther functioned as an "end times" apostle who confronted the tyranny of the Roman Catholic papacy as Antichrist.[9] But after the first stirrings of the Reformation, such eschatological provisions passed away. Thus, the ministerial functions of apostle, prophet, and evangelist—if they occur at all—are fulfilled in these latter days of the church by the pastor, who has "exactly the same purpose."[10]

Cessationism

Sometimes the view that God no longer gives some of the offices (or divine gifts) bestowed upon believers is referred to as "cessationism." Cessationism can be understood in more than one way. Basically, in terms of ministry specifically, it has to do with how certain biblical phenomena are believed to have ceased in the first century, which may include the cessation of miracles, healings, and gifts of the Holy Spirit as well as the offices of apostle, prophet, and evangelist. Calvin indeed believed that the offices of apostle, prophet, and evangelist, which the Bible also describes as "gifts of the Holy Spirit," had mostly ceased after the first century, except in very exceptional cases. However, he also believed in the more general form of cessationism, namely that miracles and God's other supernatural interventions, such as healings, had ceased as well, no longer being necessary or spiritually fruitful. Calvin said, "But that gift of healing, like the rest of the miracles, which the Lord willed to be brought forth for a time, has vanished away in order to make the new preaching of the gospel marvelous forever."[11]

In arguing for the cessation of miraculous works of the Holy Spirit in life here and now, Calvin believed that he uplifted the Holy Spirit's work in inspiring the Bible. It is the Bible, and not any person or church, that primarily represents God, at least in any supernatural way after the advent of Jesus Christ and the apostolic work of the first-century Christians. God may, through the Holy Spirit, work as God wants, but God has ordained that the Holy Spirit works ordinarily through the Bible, which describes God's will for us today. Because God is sovereign and all events are decreed by God, Calvin no longer saw the need for miracles, healings, and most—if not all—of the spiritual gifts. Based upon the testimony of the Bible, the Bible alone *(sola Scriptura)* is considered sufficient for the supernatural needs that people have today, since through it God guides them into truth for interpreting and enduring the events of life.

What then are the roles of the pastors and teachers who fulfill the permanent offices of ministry? Calvin said that pastors are responsible to preach and administer the sacraments. In addition, they are responsible for discipline, especially of church members. Pastors are thought to be responsive to a divine calling upon their lives—a "secret call," which must be confirmed by the church.[12] Pastoral ministry is for men only; Calvin rejected that there exists "an extraordinary remedy required by dire necessity," which would permit women to serve formally in church leadership.[13]

To assist in ministry, teachers (or doctors) are to instruct believers in the Christian faith. This was the ministerial function to which Calvin was primarily committed. In description of the teaching office, Calvin said, "[T]eachers are not put in charge of discipline, or administering the sacraments, but only of Scriptural interpretation—to keep doctrine whole and pure among believers."[14] Among the various ministries in which he invested time, Calvin was especially adept in Christian education. Most notably, he wrote a *Catechism of the Church of Geneva, Being a Form of Instruction for Children.* Although the catechism was particularly useful for the instruction of children, it helped people of all ages to learn more easily about Reformed beliefs, values, and practices. In further support of his teaching ministry, Calvin founded a *collège* and an *académie.* The collège educated thousands of children of elementary school age, and the *académie* educated advanced students. Both educational institutions continue to this day as the Collège Calvin and the University of Geneva, respectively.

To further assist in church ministry, Calvin discussed two additional permanent offices: elders (or governors) and deacons. First, elders were chosen from the laity to share in leadership, which included the disciplining of members of the church. Some elders taught, and some did not. Their primary role was to govern over the well-being of the church and its ministries. Second, deacons were appointed to care for the practical matters of the church, including care for the poor as well as for members of the congregation. Thus, despite some qualifications, Calvin generally talked about there being four offices that permanently represent the ministry of the church: pastors, teachers, elders, and deacons. This leadership structure was thought to endure in fulfilling the various ministries of the church. Although Luther had advocated the priesthood of all believers, Calvin's approach to church and ministry placed the chief emphasis upon the authority of the pastors, teachers, and elders to lead in sustaining the work of God's mission in the world.

Wesley's View of Ministry

Wesley was a loyal Anglican throughout his entire life. He believed that ministry took place through the superintending of the Church of England, which was governmentally episcopal in structure. Wesley was ordained at age twenty-three, and then worked as a tutor at Oxford University. He performed all the duties of the clergy, preaching and presiding over the sacraments. Like the Continental reformers, Anglicans affirmed two sacraments: baptism and the Lord's Supper. After a brief stint as a missionary to the American colony of Georgia, Wesley had his Aldersgate experience. Soon thereafter the Methodist revival began. Early on, it included open-air preaching, to which the evangelist George Whitefield introduced Wesley, before Whitefield left for the American colonies. Although at first repelled by the idea of preaching outside the doors of a church building, Wesley later helped to convert thousands of people. He famously said, "I look upon *all the world as my parish*," when Anglican leaders challenged him with regard to why he pursued such a nontraditional ministry.[15]

As the Methodist revival grew, Wesley recognized the need for discipling new (and existing) believers in ways that conventional church ministries failed to accomplish. Over time he developed a variety of Christian conferences (or small groups), based primarily upon the spiritual needs of laity. Wesley began with midweek gatherings that he called "Methodist societies." They functioned much like midweek services held in churches today. But at the time, midweek services were avant-garde, and they helped meet the needs of Christians desiring more intimate fellowship in worship and ministry opportunities than were available in churches on Sunday mornings.

To the Methodist societies, Wesley added class meetings, which allowed men and women more intimate fellowship and accountability for those interested in practicing the various means of grace. Again, Wesley believed that God instituted a variety of means of grace in the Bible, including prayer, Bible study, fasting, and ministry to the poor. Class meetings consisted of about ten to twenty Christians, and provided a fruitful context for spiritual growth and ministry. Eventually, for those especially committed to holy living, Wesley developed bands (or select societies) of fewer than ten same-gender members, which consisted of small groups of men and small groups of women. The members held one another to high degrees of spiritual accountability, asking one another intimate spiritual questions each week. When Wesley said that there is "no holiness but social holiness," he meant that holy living did not readily occur without corporate fellowship and accountability.[16] Just as Jesus Christ intimately nurtured the disciples in a small group, Wesley was convinced that the various gatherings he organized were crucial to Christians' spiritual growth as well as to effective ministry. Indeed the various small groups were the main way that Methodists ministered through evangelism, discipleship, and ministries of compassion.

Wesley did not set out to challenge the status quo of the Church of England. Indeed he tried to cooperate with Anglican leadership, as best he could, throughout his life. Be that as it may, Wesley did not cringe from challenging the ecclesiastical status quo if he believed that there existed genuine ministerial needs. Wesley's desire to minister led to the experimentation he exhibited in open-air preaching, development of Christian conferences, and focus on holy living. Wesley wanted to empower ministry in any way that he could, and that goal required willingness to assess the cultural context of society, as well as that of people, and then respond in ways that were creative as well as faithful to biblical Christianity.

Part of what drove Wesley's creative ministerial practices was his belief in the imminent presence and active work of the Holy Spirit. Unlike Calvin, Wesley did not think that the Bible contained the main depositum of the Holy Spirit's involvement in the world today. On the contrary, the Holy Spirit gives "spiritual gifts" as well as "spiritual fruit" to believers, which they are expected to use in whatever way they can in expressions of love to God and to others.[17] Wesley was far from being cessationist; instead, his views were more like what has been called, theologically speaking, "continuationism." Of course, Wesley did not use this kind of theological jargon, but he certainly thought that the Holy Spirit wants to work actively today in and through the lives of believers—to empower them in ministry.

Sometimes Wesley shocked people because of his resourceful approaches to ministry, which the direness of life circumstances necessitated. As mentioned in a previous chapter, Wesley faced an unusual state of affairs in the American colonies after the Revolutionary War. During the war, the British government had removed Anglican pastors, and the new United States of America lacked pastors to lead the many vacant churches. Since Methodist leaders had faithfully attended Anglican churches, they often took over leadership of local congregations. As Methodist influence increased in the fledgling country, Wesley oversaw the appointment of pastors and, eventually, bishops in the newly founded Methodist Episcopal Church, on account of the need for pastoral leadership. Of course, the Church of England was unhappy with several of Wesley's novel ecclesiastical decisions. But Wesley believed that extraordinary circumstances required extraordinary decisions, and he was willing to make them if others failed to do so. In time, Wesley as well as Methodism received acceptance and approval by the Church of England, even if begrudgingly so.

113

Empowering Leadership

One of Wesley's greatest contributions to ministry was the appointment of lay ministers, who led most of the Methodist Christian conferences. Since the conferences arose separately from the ecclesiastical structures of the Church of England, Wesley empowered laity to give primary leadership in the ministries. Moreover, the growth of the Methodist revivals had been remarkable; there were not enough ordained ministers available to care for everyone. As a result, some lay ministers became itinerant travelers from one Methodist society to the next, ministering to the various needs of the small groups. In particular, lay ministers were instrumental in the evangelization and discipleship of new converts to Christianity. If ordained pastors were needed among the Methodists, for example, for official ministerial and sacramental duties, then Wesley would send them to the respective societies.

Perhaps one of the boldest practices that Wesley inaugurated was the appointment of women as lay leaders. This was unprecedented in church history, and Wesley was well aware of the potential controversy it would bring upon the Methodist revival. Encouraged by his mother, Susanna Wesley, he appointed women leaders in the societies, since Wesley thought that the gifts and talents of the Holy Spirit were bestowed upon women as well as men. The Bible contained teachings that seemed to prohibit women in church leadership, yet upon reexamination of the biblical texts, Wesley thought that the trajectory of teachings on the topic of women in leadership supported their empowerment to formal ministry. Women lay leaders responded to the opportunity, and effective ministry occurred through women who led other women in the class meetings and bands.

Wesley gave tremendous leadership in caring for the poor throughout his life. Christian social activism was not unique to Wesley, but care for the poor has too often in church history been neglected in church ministries. Wesley thought, however, that there should be special preference for ministering to the poor—"Christ's poor"—based on the hundreds of verses in the Bible that command care for them.[18] He emphasized ministries of compassion from the early beginnings of the Holy Club in Oxford, which preceded the Methodist revival. Compassion ministries included the provision of food, clothing, and money for the poor; visiting prisoners; the founding of an orphanage; and low-cost education for children.

To Wesley, the poor included more than those who were financially challenged. It included anyone who was challenged physically, socially, and politically. Prisoners, for example, were those who, yes, were guilty of crimes. But they suffered inhumanely and unnecessarily because of atrocious conditions in British prisons. Wesley also became indignant about the slave trade. People ought not to enslave others, forcing slaves to endure unsanitary living conditions, families torn apart, physical abuse, and recurrent instances of death to those who resisted.

In addition to compassion ministries that care for the symptoms of poverty and injustice, advocacy ministries care for the causes of their impoverishment. Accordingly, Wesley engaged in advocacy on behalf of prison reform and abolition. For example, he published a tract called *Thoughts upon Slavery*, in which Wesley said, "Liberty is the right of every human creature, as soon as he breathes the vital air; and no human law can deprive him of that right which he derives from the law of nature."[19] In his last known letter, Wesley wrote to the abolitionist William Wilberforce, encouraging the latter to continue his work in British Parliament to change the laws that enslave and traffic in human lives.[20]

Final Thoughts

Both Wesley and Calvin challenged the status quo, so to speak, in their respective ministries. Calvin, along with other reformers, opposed the ecclesiastical hegemony of Roman Catholicism, triumphing over the Catholic beliefs, values, and practices of his time and place that departed from general Christian orthodoxy. However, he also preserved the status quo of Reformed theology that he had inherited, in large part, from Zwingli and other Swiss reformers who preceded him. In so doing, Calvin helped to establish many churches, particularly in the Reformed Protestant tradition, through his persistent apologetics and polemics against those who disagreed with his view of orthodoxy both inside and outside Protestantism. Similarly, Wesley could be said to have preserved the status quo of Anglicanism, since he did not set out to be biblically or ecclesiastically innovative. Yet, in response to the needs of people and society, Wesley challenged how Christians viewed religious experience, if nothing else, in assessing contemporary culture and then responding to it in ways that biblically ministered to the needs of all, individually and collectively. Wesley creatively responded to the spiritual and physical needs of people while remaining faithful to the gospel.

Although both contributed to the ministry of churches, Wesley and Calvin went about it in notably different ways. Calvin approached ministry in a more top-down, authoritarian, perhaps even triumphalist way that focused upon maintaining the church by means of a set-apart leadership specifically educated for preaching and administering the sacraments. His main concerns had more to do with preserving theological fidelity to the Bible, as understood by the Reformed tradition—through word and sacrament—than with creatively ministering to the needs of diverse people. Thus, Calvin spent a large part of his time proclaiming and defending orthodoxy, and polemicizing against those who disagreed with the Reformed interpretation of orthodox Christian tradition. Polemics and apologetics certainly are needed in the church, but their predominance ministerially can be problematic. Again, Calvin's approach to ministry largely had to do with maintaining the purity of proclamation of the gospel and administration of the sacraments, but it occurred in a rather controlling way. He emphasized pastors and teachers as guardians of people through a disciplinarianism that discouraged questioning and innovative solutions to people's needs other than through wide-ranging theological education.

Conversely, Wesley approached ministry in a way that was more widely embracing of innovative, yet biblically sound, ways of meeting the needs of people and society. By empowering the laity as well as clergy, including the empowerment of women in leadership, Wesley vastly expanded the ministries through which churches minister, including ministry to those who are impoverished physically as well as spiritually. In all of these ministerial matters, Wesley believed that he was not only faithful to the Bible, but that he also embodied God's mission through openness to the ongoing presence and power of the Holy Spirit.

Discussion Questions

1. How do you understand the nature of Christian ministry?

2. How does Calvin contribute to an understanding of Christian ministry? How do you like his emphasis on preaching and administering the sacraments? On church discipline? On apologetics and polemics?

3. In what ways does Calvin's view of ministry seem authoritarian, "top-down," and triumphal?

4. How does Wesley contribute to Christian ministry? How do you like his emphasis on Christian conferences, or small groups? Have you benefited from small accountability groups?

5. In what ways does Wesley's view of ministry seem empowering to laity? To women? To whom else?

6. What would be helpful today in order to improve church ministries? What ministerial practices should change or be eliminated? What ministerial practices should be added?

Conclusion:
Bringing Belief in
Line with Practice

And the crowds asked him [Jesus], "What then should we do?" (Luke 3:10)

I want to remind readers that the purpose of this book has been to affirm the beliefs, values, and practices of John Wesley, and not to put down those of John Calvin. Wesley was—and continues to be—an astute biblical interpreter, theological thinker, and church leader, who is not always well understood. There are a variety of reasons for this. It is not because Wesleyan and Methodist traditions have not grown numerically. Indeed, church growth has been significant throughout the world since the time of Wesley, and his influence continues to inspire Christians and churches. However, Wesley has not always been followed, in part because of a perceived lack of systematic theological sophistication.

However, the systematic nature of Calvin's theology is well known, and it has rightfully had a powerful impact upon the biblical and theological studies of Christians and churches worldwide. In fact, among Protestants, probably no one has had greater impact upon the intellectual development of Christianity than Calvin. His *Institutes of the Christian Religion* alone represents one of the most influential Christian books in church history.

Despite the excellence of Calvin's systematic theology, I maintain that most Christians do not live the way that he conceptualized Christianity in his life and writings. This incongruity includes many who call themselves Calvinists or who are part of the Reformed tradition that follow Calvin. Why is this incongruity the case? It is, in part, attributed to the fact that some Christians value the intellectual or conceptual uniformity of a theological system more than how they actually live out such a system in practice. But life in general can be messy, and the Christian life in particular is filled with more spiritual

117

mysteries than can finally be systematized, humanly speaking. In order to compensate for the messiness of Christianity, people are drawn to what appears to be a logically self-contained theology, even though they live in ways quite different from the logic of their stated beliefs and values. Such people are not necessarily hypocrites—that is, they do not intend to be. But they may often experience tension (or a sense of disconnect) between their beliefs and practices, or between what elsewhere I describe as the tension between theory and practice. After all, it is difficult to be a Christian in the abstract without being able to reconcile—consciously, much less subconsciously—why our beliefs and values seem so out of touch with life as we know it.

To such people, I encourage reexamination of the Bible as well as oneself. As appealing as systematic theology can be, with its claim to have a logical explanation for all the questions one might ask, how appealing can systematic theology be if it does not match all that the Bible has to say about God and salvation, and also if it does not match how one actually lives?

Bringing More Than Belief in Line with Practice

I wrote this book in order to say that Wesley presented biblical Christianity and the Christian life in ways far more like the way Christians live than did Calvin. If believers, especially those who are Protestants, want to bring their beliefs and values more in line with how they live, then they would do well to look more to Wesley than Calvin. What Wesley lacked in system development, he made up for in practice with fruitful faith development and ministry development.

Too many people live what Socrates described as the "unexamined life"; in response, he challenged people, "Know yourself!" The same can be said of Christians. Those who claim to follow either Wesley or Calvin may do so out of upbringing, habit, or intellectual laziness. Of course, becoming reflective of one's moral and faith development is also related to one's psychological and cognitive development. Be that as it may, I encourage Christians to think more about what they believe and its relationship to the best of how they live in practice. Let me ask: Do your beliefs support your practices, or do your beliefs confuse and thwart you more than they provide clarity and support? It is difficult, I realize, to consider the prospect of changing one's beliefs. Change always takes us out of our "comfort zones," so to speak. Yet, life involves taking risks every day, and the theological issues discussed in this book are too important to ignore. They demand that we become more intentional about bringing the authenticity and validity of our Christian practices in line with our beliefs and values.

Now, of course, some readers may agree that people live more like the way that Wesley described Christianity than did Calvin. But, they would ask, "Is that not the problem? Christians live more like Wesley than Calvin!" In particular, followers of Calvin might argue that followers of Wesley inadequately take into consideration, theologically speaking, the sovereignty of God or the total depravity of humanity. Well, perhaps that is the case, if you believe that Calvin's system of belief supersedes all other biblical and real-life considerations. Certainly the cognitive excellence of Calvin's systematic theology has been, historically speaking, the strongest argument for affirming Reformed theology. However, I am not convinced that Christianity is primarily a matter of the head, vis-à-vis the heart. To be sure, there is a cognitive dimension to be found in Wesley, just as there is an affective dimension found in Calvin. But I argue that Wesley holds together the importance of head and heart better than does Calvin.

Both Wesley and Calvin claimed to be biblical, to be sure. But they also interpreted crucial parts of the Bible differently. For example, I have contended that Calvin conceived of the Christian faith more in terms of intellectual excellence, truth, and doctrine, whereas Wesley conceived of the Christian faith more in terms of relational excellence, love, and empowerment. This does not mean that Calvin was not concerned with relational excellence, love, and empowerment, and that Wesley was not concerned with intellectual excellence, truth, and doctrine. But Wesley was more relational in orientation than was Calvin; love and empowerment to grow spiritually were stronger in Wesley than in Calvin. One way I put it in the book was that Calvin was more *orthodoxy* (right beliefs) oriented, whereas Wesley was more *orthopraxy* (right actions) and *orthokardia* (right hearts) oriented. To be sure, this comparison has more to do with emphases than either-or categorical distinctions. But different emphases often make all the difference in terms of how we understand our Christianity as well as our relationship with God, with ourselves, and with others, individually and societally.

Eight Reasons

In this book, I present eight chapters comparing and contrasting Wesley and Calvin. In a sense, I provide eight reasons Wesley is a more representative and persuasive spokesperson for biblical Christianity and the Christian life than is Calvin. Of course, there are other ways that Wesley and Calvin may be contrasted, and of course, there are still other ways that they may be compared in agreeing with each other. Indeed, they agree with each other more than they disagree. But it is in their disagreements that we discover what made Wesley and Calvin both unique and also influential among subsequent Christians. Thus we need to focus on these distinguishing characteristics more than anything else, in order to evaluate how influential they should be in terms of how we believe, value, and practice today as Christians.

Let us consider again the eight reasons Wesley is a more representative spokesperson for biblical Christianity and the Christian life than is Calvin. The following represents a summary of the eight aforementioned chapters.

1. God: More Love Than Sovereignty

Both Wesley and Calvin believed in the sovereign power and majesty of God. But Calvin put so much emphasis upon the power, providence, and predestination of God that he undermined other divine attributes. Wesley emphasized the love of God in how God relates with humanity. God's love does not negate God's power, majesty, and glory; such divine attributes should be thought to affirm people's potential for relationship with God, rather than undermine it. After all, God wants to redeem people from sin in order that they may become personally reconciled with God. For Wesley, it is important for people to think of God as a loving parent—one who cares for us with the best qualities of parenthood in mind. A parent remains strong and awe-inspiring, especially in relationship to children when they are young. But more than anything else, a parent wants to increase in relationship with children as they grow and mature, just as God wants to be in loving relationship with us.

How do you view God? How you conceive of God significantly affects how you live your life here and now as well as how you relate spiritually with God. Do you view God as an all-powerful being whose transcendent majesty and glory surpasses all understanding? Some people have that image of God, but such a transcendent view—as grand and awe-inspiring as it is—may be excessive, thus thwarting any hope for relationship with a God too far removed from them. Without denying the sovereignty of God, Wesley emphasized how important it is to conceive of God in terms of love, grace, mercy, forgiveness, and transformation. Such a conception does not negate God's holiness, righteousness, justice, and judgment. All of the aforementioned attributes are important for how we conceive of God; the same could be said of how we conceive of God as a parent, considering the best of parenthood. But Wesley believed that both the Bible and experience emphasize the steadfast love of God as preeminent for a healthy conception of and relationship with God.

120

2. Bible: More Primary Than Sole Authority

Calvin's view of biblical authority has been described as *sola Scriptura*—Scripture only. It is true that the Bible represented his primary religious authority, though Calvin studied the Bible in light of historic Christian scholarship as well as logical, systematic reasoning. Wesley, however, developed his biblical studies through the Anglican tradition, which emphasized the primacy of biblical authority along with the genuine religious authority of church tradition and critical thinking. To these religious authorities, Wesley added experience, which included personal religious experience and other experiences of a social and scientific nature. He did not think that he was doing anything theologically innovative; instead, Wesley thought that he was making explicit what Christians had always done, namely, take a contextual approach to theology and ministry, with the Bible as their primary religious authority.

How do you make theological, ethical, and ministry decisions? Do you use the Bible only? Or, is your decision-making process more complex, utilizing a variety of considerations—past, present, and future—in understanding and applying the Bible to real-life questions, concerns, and obligations? To Wesley, it was naive to think that the Bible was the only religious authority to which Christians could appeal. Thus, it is not a matter of *if* but *when* other religious authorities come into play in our decision making. Rather than perpetuate the myth of using the Bible only, Wesley considered it wiser to decide how the various religious authorities ought to be utilized, so long as biblical authority remains primary.

3. Humanity: More Freedom Than Predestination

Calvin's belief in divine sovereignty emphasized God's all-powerful governance of the affairs of people. God decreed before the foundation of the world a plan for creation and for people. God's decrees are inviolable. Thus, people—who are both finite and sinful—must humbly submit to God's providential care in all that occurs in life. After all, by themselves, people are incapable of achieving anything of eternal significance. But thanks be to God; since God elects some people for salvation, they may be redeemed from their totally depraved state of existence.

Wesley agreed that people are sinful and cannot save themselves. Salvation occurs by grace through faith. However, the faith that people have represents an act of uncoerced volition. By means of the prevenient grace of God, people may choose to accept God's gift of salvation, or choose to reject it. Calvin, however, conceived of faith as that which is compatible with God's will. People cannot possibly thwart God, since that would represent a diminishment of

God's sovereignty. Wesley did not agree. He did not think that God's sovereignty precluded God from self-limiting God's power over people so that they may genuinely decide to choose or reject the offer of eternal life. Such a decision may be initiated, enabled, and completed by divine grace. Yet, Wesley believed that people can and must make decisions of their own free will (or free grace, as Wesley preferred to call it) in this life. So our decisions here and now become extremely important; some of them have eternal significance. In fact, people have freedom with regard to many matters in life. As such, they ought not to think that their futures are so set by divine command that they are without responsibility or hope for decisions they make here and now.

4. Grace: More Prevenient Than Irresistible

God works graciously in the lives of people. Grace represents divine favor as well as empowerment for salvation and for Christian living. Calvin affirmed the Reformation principles of salvation by grace alone (*sola gratia*) and faith alone (*sola fide*). He considered divine grace to be effectual—that is, people cannot resist God's work in their lives for their justification, sanctification, and glorification. Because of people's finitude and sin, God must be viewed as the overarching cause of people's spiritual well-being, since people can do nothing to merit or earn their eternal life.

Wesley also believed in salvation by grace through faith. However, he believed that divine grace was conditional. That is, God does not work irresistibly in the lives of people. Instead, God chooses to work preveniently in relationship to people. Prevenient grace enables people freedom to choose justification, sanctification, and other matters in life. God indeed elects people to salvation, but election is based upon divine foreknowledge, rather than upon irresistible decrees of God determined before the foundation of the world. People may not have complete freedom of choice, since they are still hampered by human finitude and sin; moreover, their free will is not a natural potentiality, since people's choices are enabled by God's prevenient grace. But people have constant access to divine grace through the presence of work of the Holy Spirit. Therefore, they need to be attentive to God's Spirit as well as to the Bible and Christian teaching, since God enables them to have a genuine measure of freedom to choose salvation, to love God, and to love their neighbor as themselves.

5. Salvation: More Unlimited Than Limited

Calvin believed that, given the dire circumstances of sinful humanity, God so loved the world that provision was made for people's atonement through the life, death, and resurrection of Jesus Christ. Jesus represented a substitute for sinners, and through him salvation is made possible. Those whom God elected for eternal life before the foundation of the world receive the benefit of Jesus' atonement. Followers of Calvin affirmed the substitutionary atonement, but thought that it must be limited only for the elect. Although Calvin did not explicitly affirm theological belief in limited atonement, the implication appears throughout his writings. Since God elects some for salvation and reprobates others for damnation for eternity, Jesus' atonement cannot logically be understood as having been universally offered to all people. Calvin tried to balance a belief in universal atonement in Christ with particular election, but ultimately it is God—not people—who determines who are saved and who are damned.

Wesley, however, was appalled at any prospect of limiting atonement. He strongly affirmed that Jesus lived, died, and was resurrected on behalf of everyone. Such universality does not imply universal salvation, because people still need to respond, by grace, to God's offer of redemption. God offers salvation to all, but only those who by grace through faith accept God's offer will be saved. To Wesley, it seemed both theologically suspect and ministerially cruel for Calvin to proclaim salvation to those for whom it is impossible to be saved, because of God's predetermination of their reprobation. Instead, Wesley urgently proclaimed the gospel message, in order that people might respond by grace in fulfillment of the salvific conditions of faith and repentance.

6. Spirituality: More Holiness Than Mortification

Calvin believed that God accomplished justification and sanctification in the lives of believers. God accomplished these feats of salvation by grace, and not through the merits or contributions of people. Calvin's emphasis on the third use of the law distinguished him from Luther, since Calvin placed more emphasis on the need to live obediently in accordance with God's law. God uses the law both to mortify and vivify believers through their obedience. Mortification reminds people that their salvation is a gift, and they contribute nothing to it; vivification spiritually enlivens and consoles them in their humble submission to God. Their spiritual growth occurs according to the decrees and will of God, not by any human contribution. In this life, believers are both saved and sinful. But by God's grace, they may be sustained through the struggles of life as they also mortify their lives through obedience to biblical teaching, in hope of God's vivification.

Wesley was far more hopeful about the degree to which God wants to engage people in their spiritual formation and the degree to which they may live holy, Christlike lives. After conversion, God's Holy Spirit continues to work graciously in the lives of believers, prompting them to repent of ongoing sin and to consecrate their lives wholly to the lordship of Jesus Christ. Indeed, Wesley generally thought that at some point, subsequent to conversion, believers faced the crisis of submitting their entire lives to Jesus' lordship. God meets this consecration with grace for their entire sanctification. Believers do not become absolutely perfect; however, they may grow more effectively by the grace of God. Wesley was very hopeful about the degree to which God wants people to partner with the Holy Spirit in their spiritual formation and in living holy, Christlike lives.

7. Church: More Catholic Than Magisterial

Calvin had high regard for the church, and saw the need to keep it pure from defects, based upon the teachings of the Bible. In keeping the church pure, it was necessary to engage in ongoing apologetics and polemics against those who challenged Christianity, in general, and Reformed theology, in particular. Opposition needed to be censured, excommunicated, banished, or perchance executed. Such disciplinarianism required a union between the church and civil government, since the latter was thought to be divinely appointed to conserve the juridical and punitive order of both ecclesiastical and civil laws. Calvin's authoritarian leadership over the church, coupled with the all-embracing governance of civil magistrates over every aspect of people's lives, reflects the magisterial nature of Calvin's view of the church in the world.

Wesley had a far more catholic, or irenic, view of how Christians and churches ought to relate with each other. He did not fail to emphasize the importance of biblical and orthodox teachings in the church. However, Wesley thought that churches ought to be more inclusive and cooperative with other Christians, rather than being quick to judge and condemn them. In his conception of the church, Wesley thought that it was important to emphasize heart religion along with right beliefs. As such, it is important to emphasize a right heart and right actions as well as right relations with others. Faithful living coupled with faithful believing was crucial to the life and ministry of churches. Thus, aligning churches with civil government too closely was biblically and theologically problematic. Wesley emphasized more of a separation of church and state than did Calvin, since the church could be too easily co-opted by governmental influence that was not beneficial for either the church or government.

8. Ministry: More Empowering Than Triumphal

Calvin emphasized the ministry of preaching the word of God—the Bible—and the right administration of the sacraments. "Word and sacrament" became a theme of his ministry. Enforcing discipline was also important, and Calvin placed great emphasis upon how both the church and civil authorities were ordained to regulate the words and actions of people. In churches, pastors and teachers are to take the lead in proclaiming God's sovereign majesty as well as the primacy of biblical teachings, since the Bible embodies much of the work of the Holy Spirit today. Ministry extended beyond churches into service that uplifted theological education and the spread of the Reformed understanding of biblical Christianity. Such ministries served to announce God's sovereign triumph over the world as well as Calvin's representation of it.

Wesley emphasized a more creative, evangelistic, conference-oriented, and empowering approach to ministry. He affirmed biblical emphases upon preaching and administering sacraments in churches, but he also pioneered innovative ministries based upon the complex needs of people. Such innovations included field preaching, and the development of small group ministries consisting of Methodist societies, class meetings, and bands. The latter were designed to be the heart of making disciples and of ministry toward others. Wesley did not shy away from responding to the direst needs of people, for example, when he founded the Methodist Episcopal Church in the newly created United States, since the Church of England had withdrawn its ministers. Finally, Wesley thought that ministry should be directed especially on behalf of the poor. It was not enough, however, to provide only compassion ministries that dealt with the symptoms of impoverishment. Wesley also engaged in advocacy ministries that dealt with the causes of impoverishment, for example, working on behalf of prison reform and the abolition of slavery.

More Wesley, Less Calvin

In any given instance above, readers might say that they agree with Calvin more than Wesley. However, given the accumulation of reasons, I think that more Christians—particularly Protestant Christians—would agree with Wesley than with Calvin. Even those who claim to be from the Reformed tradition would likely have difficulty agreeing with Calvin more than Wesley, when considering all dimensions of their view of the Bible and Christian living.

Some people simply do not care, or do not feel a need to decide about such matters. Sometimes people with whom I speak call themselves "Cal-minian," stating that they like both *Cal*-vinist and Ar-*minian* beliefs. Usually such a comment is made in order to be humorous or to avoid theological discussion. To be sure, one's salvation certainly is not dependent upon whether one sides more with the likes of Wesley or of Calvin. However, I still agree with Socrates: the unexamined life is not worth living. And the more that people bring their Christian beliefs and values in line with their practices, the more established and effective they will be.

No doubt some will have difficulty acknowledging that their beliefs and values (as well as their actions) indeed resemble Wesley more than Calvin. It is difficult for people to change, even when change helps them become more knowledgeable, confident, and mature in their Christian living. Be that as it may, I encourage people to decide for themselves whether they think, speak, and act more like Wesley than Calvin.

My conclusion: more Wesley, and less Calvin. This is not to say that we cannot still learn a great deal from Calvin. We can, and we should! However, if you want to become more intentional about conceptualizing your Christian beliefs in ways that fortify—rather than weaken—biblical teachings and your Christian living, then I strongly encourage you to learn about, reflect upon, and then follow Wesley's theology and ministry.

What Then Should We Do?

I love the story of John the Baptist, told in Luke 3:1-14. John, who was the cousin of Jesus, began to preach throughout first-century Judea, proclaiming that people ought to repent and be baptized. Some repented and were baptized by John in the Jordan River. Others reviled him, since John also claimed to "prepare the way of the Lord"—the coming Messiah (Luke 3:4).

Those in the crowd who believed, asked John: "What then should we do?" (Luke 3:10). John did not give merely spiritual responses, such as pray more, worship on the Sabbath, study the Scriptures, and so on. Instead, John gave tangible, ethical responses that required commitment and self-sacrifice on the part of the crowd. He said that people were to share their wealth with the poor; he said that tax collectors should not unjustly collect taxes from people; and he said that soldiers should not extort money from anyone by threats or false accusations.

When I think of this story, I am reminded of how important it is to live realistically as Christians and not just think that we have done enough if we claim to have a right set of biblical and theological beliefs. Wesley thought that biblical and theological beliefs are important, but he also thought that people's beliefs ought to be brought in line with their practices, just as people's practices ought to be brought in line with their beliefs and values. It is not an either-or concern; instead, it is a "both-and" concern that emphasizes the importance of *both* beliefs *and* practices, values *and* their applications. Wesley, I argue, was masterful at holding together beliefs and practices that others rejected, since they could not develop a sufficiently systematized understanding, at least of Christianity. But systematization—as intellectually appealing as it is—fails to do justice to the complexities and challenges of the Bible and of life physically and socially as well as spiritually. Wesley integrated Christian beliefs and values in line with practice better than did Calvin, and I encourage people to decide for themselves with regard to how they may best integrate their Christianity in line with their practice.

Discussion Questions

1. After having read this book, who best speaks on behalf of how you both believe and act as a Christian: Wesley or Calvin?

2. What aspects of Calvin's beliefs, values, and practices do you consider to be the most persuasive?

3. What aspects of Wesley's beliefs, values, and practices do you consider to be the most persuasive?

4. What Christian beliefs discussed in this book would you like to investigate further?

5. What Christian practices—personal practices and collective church practices—would you like to investigate further?

6. What is your response to the crowd's question to John the Baptist: "What then should we do?"

7. To put the question another way, what then should you do?

Appendix: More ACURA Than TULIP

For those whom he foreknew he also predestined to be conformed to the image of his Son, in order that he might be the firstborn within a large family.
(Romans 8:29)

John Calvin prominently influenced the development of Reformed theology. His followers produced several statements of faith, some during the life of Calvin and some after his death. Prominent examples include the Gallic Confession (1559), Scots Confession (1560), Second Helvetic Confession (1562), Heidelberg Catechism (1563), Belgic Confession (1566), Canons of Dort (1619), Westminster Confession of Faith (1646), and so on.

In the Netherlands, the Dutch Reformed Church wanted to unify churches around consensual doctrines. A synod (or conference) was convened in the city of Dort (or Dordt, Dordrecht) in 1618, which included Reformed representatives from eight additional European countries. The Synod of Dort endorsed three Reformed statements of faith: Heidelberg Catechism, Belgic Confession, and the Decision of the Synod of Dort on the Five Main Points of Doctrine in Dispute in the Netherlands. The latter document summarized the conclusions of the synod, which are popularly known as the "Canons of Dort." Sometimes these collective documents have been referred to as the "Three Forms of Unity," which became foundational for the doctrine of many Reformed churches.

Although the Synod of Dort discussed many issues, there were "five main points of doctrine" that the followers of Jacobus Arminius (1560–1609) disputed. Arminius had been a leader among Dutch Reformed Christians. He and his followers challenged the strongly predestinarian beliefs of Calvinism, appealing to prevenient grace as the divine means by which God enables people to have a measure of choice with regard to accepting or rejecting God's gift of salvation. After Arminius's death in 1609, his followers submitted the

128

Five Articles of the Remonstrance (protest, or disagreement) in 1610 to the states of Holland and Friesland. The articles argued point by point on behalf of Arminianism, especially regarding divine predestination and human freedom. The five points became a topic of much debate in the Netherlands; this threatened the unity of Reformed churches. Thus, the Synod of Dort was convened. The followers of Arminius—known as "Remonstrants"—came to the synod in 1618 expecting an opportunity to argue for their theological views; instead, their views were declared anathema. That is, their views were denounced, and those who promoted Arminian beliefs were banished or persecuted. Some were killed. Consequently, Arminians fled the Netherlands and went to other European countries, especially Britain and eventually the American colonies.

The five points are often used to summarize the differences between Calvinists and Arminians. Basically they are doctrines that have to do with different views about the degree to which God determines or permits events to occur, especially with regard to salvation. And the reason the debate is important to the topic of this book is because the beliefs of Arminius were similar to those of Wesley. As stated earlier, it does not appear that Arminius significantly influenced Wesley in the development of Wesley's theology and ministry. But in his later life, Wesley identified with the moniker of "Arminian" in his growing debates with Calvinists. For example, Wesley published the *Arminian Magazine,* which contained articles that promoted Methodism and contrasted Wesley's views with those of Calvin. Wesley's identification with Arminianism was a popularly known way of distinguishing between two of the more prominent Protestant views of divine predestination and human freedom; it helped provide theological categories for longstanding debate on the topic, and association with Arminius's theology no doubt gave Wesley's views added credibility.

Calvin, Arminius, and Wesley

The views of Arminius and Wesley were not, historically speaking, new to them. Several times in this book I have talked about how they embodied the majority of views held by Christians since the time of the apostles. The views of Augustine, Luther, and Calvin do not represent the way most Christians in church history viewed the relationship between divine predestination and human freedom. This is a historical misnomer that often confuses Christians, given the apparent prominence of Calvin's theology, at least among Protestants. Instead, Arminian-oriented views most closely resembled those of Roman Catholicism, Orthodox churches, Anglicans, and others who represented the majority theological view in church history.

The same is true of the majority of Christians today; most hold Arminian-oriented views, even if they do so primarily in practice, rather than in theory (or theology). Like their theological forebears, Arminius and Wesley tried to counter what they considered to be excesses in the biblical understanding of Augustinian (and later Lutheran and Calvinist) views of the sovereignty of God. Sovereignty did not mean that people are without a significant and thus responsible amount of human freedom. On the contrary, God's sovereignty enables people by grace to respond to God in faith and thus become reconciled with God. People are saved by grace through faith; likewise, by grace God permits people freedom to respond in faith, despite the ongoing effects of finitude and sin in their lives.

Earlier I talked about how these rival viewpoints are best categorized as Augustinianism (for example, Luther and Calvin) and Semi-Augustinianism (for example, Thomas Aquinas, Arminius, and Wesley). (See chapter 3, "Humanity: More Freedom than Predestination.") It is not a difference between Augustinianism and Pelagianism (or even Semi-Pelagianism), since the latter believe that people must initiate their salvation, thus resembling a kind of works righteousness rejected by biblical authors. Semi-Augustinianism, however, believes that God permits people a measure of freedom, which is enabled by divine grace. God initiates salvation; yet God wants people to respond freely to the gift of salvation, since salvation involves the restoration of relationship with God as well as the atonement of Jesus Christ. Sin makes it impossible for people to save themselves by any natural ability, work, or merit. But God, through the presence and work of the Holy Spirit, provides preveniently sufficient grace for people to decide through faith to accept God's salvation. Such a decision is not merely compatible with God's will, but a condition required by God. It is a condition that people may reject, and by such a rejection they become culpable of sin and judgment.

Because Wesley and Calvin represent leaders of large church traditions, the two have come to epitomize the age-old debate over the relationship between divine predestination and human freedom. The problem is, however, that it is questionable whether the five points of Calvinism accurately represent Calvin. In addition, it is not clear that Arminius would have agreed with every point made by the Remonstrants. Finally, Wesley's beliefs and values do not exactly match those of either Arminius or the Remonstrants. Thus, historically and theologically, it is doubtful how adequately the five points of debate provide accurate categories for understanding Wesley and Calvin as well as Arminius. In fact, I did not use the five points as a way to compare and contrast Wesley and Calvin in this book because it would have been anachronistic as well as theologically inaccurate to do so.

Be that as it may, doctrinal discussion at the Synod of Dort touches upon many beliefs and values held by Wesley and Calvin. So, although we must qualify the preciseness with which views of the five points represent Wesley and Calvin, I will use them in this appendix to summarize key differences between the two church leaders. The five points may not be perfect criteria for comparison, but they are sufficient, at least, to help readers recognize how Wesley and Calvin disagreed with each other. For many, the core differences between the two leaders revolve—rightly or wrongly—around their respective views of divine predestination and human freedom.

The Canons of Dort and TULIP

Although the Remonstrants first articulated the five points of disagreement with Calvinism in 1610, I will begin by talking about the views decided upon by the Dutch Reformed Church when the Synod of Dort concluded in 1619, since they represent a more widely known doctrinal summary. In the Canons of Dort, the Dutch Reformed Church summarized its disagreement with the Remonstrants.

Let me present each of the five main points, using quotations from articles of the Canons of Dort, which will help clarify the core of each point. I begin with the first main point (of the five points), and summarize it by quoting from the article having to do with God's eternal decision (or decrees):

The First Main Point of Doctrine Concerning Divine Predestination

Article 6: God's Eternal Decision

The fact that some receive from God the gift of faith within time, and that others do not, stems from his eternal decision. For "all his works are known to God from eternity." In accordance with this decision he graciously softens the hearts, however hard, of his chosen ones and inclines them to believe, but by his just judgment he leaves in their wickedness and hardness of heart those who have not been chosen. And in this especially is disclosed to us his act—unfathomable, and as merciful as it is just—of distinguishing between people equally lost. This is the well-known decision of election and reprobation revealed in God's word. This decision the wicked, impure, and unstable distort to their own ruin, but it provides holy and godly souls with comfort beyond words.[1]

The aforementioned quotation refers to what later Calvinists describe as "unconditional election." It includes both of God's eternal decrees, declared before the foundation of the world, about who will be elect (saved) and who will be reprobate (damned). Although Calvin did not use the phrase *double predestination* to describe the dual decrees of those who are saved and those who are damned, his followers did—for example, Theodore Beza, who articulated the doctrine of supralapsarianism. Supralapsarianism emphasizes the sovereignty of God's decrees to save some people and to condemn others, even before God decreed to create the world and humanity.

The second main point of the Canons of Dort had to do with do with the atonement of Jesus Christ. The article quoted below has to do with the effectiveness or efficaciousness of Jesus' death:

The Second Main Point of Doctrine: Christ's Death and Human Redemption through It

Article 8: The Saving Effectiveness of Christ's Death

For it was the entirely free plan and very gracious will and intention of God the Father that the enlivening and saving effectiveness of his Son's costly death should work itself out in all his chosen ones, in order that he might grant justifying faith to them only and thereby lead them without fail to salvation.[2]

Jesus Christ provided atonement for humanity. But only chosen ones receive its "saving effectiveness."

The third and fourth main points are combined. They have to do with what came to be known as the "total depravity of humanity," and consequently with people's need for God's grace to work irresistibly in their lives. I quote from the first three articles that deal with the helplessness of humanity and how people must rely solely upon God:

The Third and Fourth Main Points of Doctrine: Human Corruption, Conversion to God, and the Way They Occur

Article 1: The Effect of the Fall on Human Nature

Man was originally created in the image of God and was furnished in his mind with a true and salutary knowledge of his Creator and things spiritual, in his will and heart with righteousness, and in all his emotions with purity; indeed, the whole man was holy. However, rebelling against God at the devil's instigation and by his own free will, he deprived himself of these outstanding gifts. Rather, in their place he brought upon himself blindness, terrible darkness, futility, and distortion of judgment in his mind; perversity, defiance, and hardness in his heart and will; and finally impurity in all his emotions.

Article 2: The Spread of Corruption

Man brought forth children of the same nature as himself after the fall. That is to say, being corrupt he brought forth corrupt children. The corruption spread, by God's just judgment, from Adam to all his descendants—except for Christ alone—not by way of imitation (as in former times the Pelagians would have it) but by way of the propagation of his perverted nature.

Article 3: Total Inability

Therefore, all people are conceived in sin and are born children of wrath, unfit for any saving good, inclined to evil, dead in their sins, and slaves to sin; without the grace of the regenerating Holy Spirit they are neither willing nor able to return to God, to reform their distorted nature, or even to dispose themselves to such reform.[3]

The fifth and final main point of the Canons of Dort has to do with the perseverance of the saints. I quote from the article that talks about how it is God who must not only save the elect but must preserve them as well:

The Fifth Main Point of Doctrine: The Perseverance of the Saints

Article 3: God's Preservation of the Converted

Because of these remnants of sin dwelling in them and also because of the temptations of the world and Satan, those who have been converted could not remain standing in this grace if left to their own resources. But God is faithful, mercifully strengthening them in the grace once conferred on them and powerfully preserving them in it to the end.[4]

In the English language, the five points of Calvinism are most often summarized by the acrostic TULIP. The acrostic does not follow the exact order as the Canons of Dort, but it has become the most common way to refer to the five points. They include:

1. Total depravity

2. Unconditional election

3. Limited atonement

4. Irresistible grace

5. Perseverance of the saints

Each of the aforementioned points of Calvinism is, at times, referred to by different terms. Sometimes the cognate terms are enlightening; sometimes they are confusing, at best, and incorrect, at worst. Consider the following examples:

1. Total depravity: total inability, total hereditary depravity, or original sin

2. Unconditional election: God's eternal decision, or God's election (cf. double predestination)

3. Limited atonement: particular atonement, particular redemption, or justification is limited

4. Irresistible grace: effectual calling, or efficacious call of the Spirit

5. Perseverance of the saints: eternal security, or once saved, always saved

I do not plan to discuss the benefits and liabilities of the various terms used above to identify the five points of Calvinism. Suffice it to say that I choose to talk about TULIP, since it is the most common way that people think about the views of Calvin and Calvinism with regard to divine predestination and human freedom, particularly in relationship to salvation.

The Remonstrance and the Five Points of Arminianism

The Remonstrance (or the Arminian Articles, 1610) was first presented as five points of disagreement with the theology of the Dutch Reformed Church. The document containing the points of disagreement is not long, and so I will quote from it at length. I want readers to learn firsthand about the Remonstrants' five concerns about Calvinist views of divine predestination and human freedom. Consider the following:

The Remonstrance

Article 1

That God, by an eternal and unchangeable purpose in Jesus Christ his Son, before the foundations of the world were laid, determined to save, out of the human race which had fallen into sin, in Christ, for Christ's sake, and

134

through Christ, those who through the grace of the Holy Spirit shall believe on the same his Son and shall through the same grace persevere in this same faith and obedience of faith even to the end; and on the other hand to leave under sin and wrath the contumacious and unbelieving and to condemn them as aliens from Christ, according to the word of the Gospel in John 3.36.

Article 2

That, accordingly, Jesus Christ the Savior of the world, died for all and for every individual, so that he has obtained for all, by his death on the cross, reconciliation and remission of sins; yet so that no one is partaker of this remission except the believers, according to the word of the Gospel of John 3.16.

Article 3

That the human has not saving grace of himself, nor of the working of his own free will, inasmuch as in his state of apostasy and sin he can for himself and by himself think nothing that is good—nothing, that is, truly good, such as saving faith is, above all else. But that it is necessary that by God, in Christ, and through his Holy Spirit he be born again and renewed in understanding, affections and will, and in all his faculties, that he may be able to understand, think, will, and perform what is truly good, according to the word of Christ, John 15.5.

Article 4

That this grace of God is the beginning, the progress, and the end of all good; so that even the regenerate human can neither think, will, nor effect any good, nor withstand any temptation to evil, without grace precedent (or prevenient), awakening, following, and cooperating. So that all deeds and all movements towards good that can be conceived in thought must be ascribed to the grace of God in Christ. But with this respect to the mode of operation, grace is not irresistible.

Article 5

That those who are grafted into Christ by a true faith, and have thereby been made partakers of his life-giving Spirit, are abundantly endowed with power to strive against Satan, sin, the world, and their own flesh, and to win the victory; always, be it understood, with the help of the grace of the Holy Spirit, with Jesus Christ assisting them in all temptations, through his Spirit; stretching out his hand to them and (providing only that they are themselves prepared for the fight, that they entreat his aid and do not fail to help themselves) propping and upbuilding them so that by no guile or violence of Satan can they be led astray or plucked from Christ's hands, according to the word of Christ, John 10. . . . But for the question whether they are not able through sloth or negligence to forsake the beginning of their life in Christ, to embrace again this present world, to depart from the holy doctrine once delivered to them, to lose their good conscience, and to neglect grace—this must be the subject of more exact inquiry in the Holy Scriptures, before we can teach it with full confidence of our mind.[5]

If I want to summarize the five points of Arminianism in a way that contrasts point by point with the five points of Calvinism, listed under the acrostic TULIP, then I could do it in the following way. I use the precise wording above, using the English translations of the Dutch theological terms:

1. Conditional predestination

2. Universal atonement

3. Saving faith

4. Resistible grace

5. The uncertainty of perseverance

As important as these terms are to describe Arminianism (as well as represent the longstanding traditions of Roman Catholicism, Orthodox churches, and Anglicanism), they are regrettably not well known. Because they are not well known, too often they have been misrepresented, maligned, or neglected for being a nonconformist biblical and theological alternative to Calvinist beliefs about divine predestination and human freedom. However, charges against them for heresy and being theologically unorthodox are wrong! Regardless of whether the charges were made out of ignorance or malevolence, the Semi-Augustinian-oriented views of Arminianism are soundly Bible based. Indeed, they represent the majority Christian view, historically speaking.

The marginalization of the views of Arminianism and Wesleyanism (as well as the views of Roman Catholicism, Orthodox churches, and Anglicanism) is in part because of the hegemony of biblical and theological scholarship representative of Lutheran and Reformed church traditions. To their credit, Lutheran and Reformed scholars have done excellent work in developing, publishing, and promoting their theologies. But, despite their scholarly success, they have not spoken for the majority of Christians, including Protestant Christians. So greater historical as well as theological awareness is needed. It is needed in order to recognize the nature and extent of Semi-Augustinian beliefs and values, reflective of Arminian and Wesleyan views about divine predestination, human freedom, and salvation.

Proper Understanding of Arminianism

Let me give some examples of how the five points of Arminianism have been misunderstood or misrepresented. (1) Conditional predestination has been caricatured as an abrogated election—that is, as a rejection of divine election altogether. But such an understanding of Arminianism is preposterous, since the Remonstrants clearly believed in election based upon God's eternal knowledge of who will accept salvation by grace through faith. God does indeed elect some for salvation, but the election is based upon God's eternal knowledge of who by grace will decide to believe in Jesus Christ—knowledge that people refer to as "foreknowledge."

(2) Arminian belief in the universality of the atonement of Jesus Christ has been caricatured as universal salvation or universalism, being falsely accused of claiming that all will be saved and that no one will be damned. However, the Remonstrants did not believe in universal salvation. They firmly believed that Jesus died for all, and not merely for the elect chosen by God, without divine foreknowledge of who would accept his salvation. Certainly some choose to reject God, according to the Remonstrants, and thus warrant culpability for sin, judgment, and damnation.

(3) Saving faith has to do with how people, on account of sin, cannot humanly or by natural means save themselves. Thus people must respond to God's grace by faith in order to be saved. However, Arminianism has been caricatured as advocating a diminished depravity that made it possible for people, humanly speaking, to earn or merit their salvation. This could not be farther from the truth, since the Remonstrants firmly believed that God initiated, enabled, and completed people's salvation. There is no hint either of works righteousness or Pelagianism in Arminian theology.

(4) With regard to divine grace, the Remonstrants believed that it was resistible. God does not coerce people to convert; instead, God gives them grace to accept or reject salvation. God graciously permits people to decide for themselves, and their decisions indeed have eternal significance. The Arminians did not believe in a sedentary or inactive grace, wherein people must rely on their own human effort or merit. Accusations to the contrary are attempts to caricature Arminianism as a variation of Pelagianism. Unfortunately, critics of the Remonstrants—past and present—have sometimes resorted to theological distortion rather than try to understand truthfully and debate fairly those with whom they disagree.

(5) In discussing the perseverance of the saints, the Remonstrants did not explicitly say that Christians could intentionally and habitually reject their salvation. What they said was that, based upon the testimony of the Bible, it

is uncertain whether those who are saved may or may not become apostate. But Arminians certainly disagreed with the Calvinists' claimed sense of certainty with regard to the perseverance of the saints, since assurance as well as salvation itself consists of an ongoing relationship with God's Holy Spirit. After all, claims to certainty are no guarantee of truth. Moreover, Calvin gave no clear-cut way for people to know for sure in this life whether they are or are not elect, since it is a matter of divine decision rather than anything people may decide.

Wesley and ACURA

Wesley did not appeal to Arminius and Arminianism during most of his life and ministry. Only later in life did Wesley identify with the established theological tradition of Arminianism. His identification occurred in the context of growing debate with Calvinists, especially over issues related to the roles of God and people regarding salvation. Although Wesley and Arminius did not entirely agree point by point, their theological views of divine predestination and human freedom were sufficiently like-minded to the extent that Wesley became the main Protestant proponent of Semi-Augustinian-oriented Arminianism in the English-speaking world.

To this day, people, in general, and Protestants, in particular, either do not know or understand the Semi-Augustinian, Arminian, and Wesleyan views of the so-called five points of the Remonstrants discussed above. As already stated, people tend to be woefully ignorant or uninformed about church history, much less the history of Christian theology. They may also be misinformed, which is especially problematic when Calvinists and others distort the beliefs of Wesley and those like him. When advocates of the Reformed tradition set out to defend their views apologetically or to attack polemically those who disagree with them, their treatment of alternative viewpoints such as Wesley's can become distorted—intentionally as well as unintentionally. Thus, it is important that Wesley's views about divine predestination and human freedom receive a fair and critical hearing, and not an unfair and uncritical dismissal.

I argue that one of the reasons Wesley (and Arminius, for that matter) does not often enough receive sufficient hearing is because his beliefs are not easily identifiable vis-à-vis those of Calvin. Let me explain. When people hear the word *TULIP*, they can more easily remember the five points of Calvinism. They may not agree with each point, at least not entirely or not entirely in practice. But, since they do not readily know an alternative, people may feel that they have no other theological options. Consequently, they sometimes have to wrestle with TULIP and decide that they may only agree with four points, three points, two points, one and a half points, or who knows what other permutation they may devise. Because they do not readily know the counterpoints of Calvinism, all they know to do is to accept, perhaps reluctantly, portions of TULIP.

Now, Wesley did not talk about the five points of Calvinism or Arminianism per se. Again, Wesley was not wedded to Arminian theology. Be that as it may, his beliefs and values were substantively the same as Arminius, at least with regard to their views of divine predestination, human freedom, and salvation. So, in my opinion, there needs to be a better way to compare and contrast the views of Wesley and Calvin than is currently available.

Thus I propose use of an acrostic that may help people to better understand the theology of Wesley, and make it easier to compare him with the five points of Calvinism. Having such a mnemonic (or memory) device will help people become more aware and appreciative of alternative views to those of Calvin and his followers. Of course, the creation of such an acrostic requires some imagination, since its success may need to be more memorable than systematic. Now, I do not intend to be either biblically or historically inaccurate. But slightly modified phraseology will help to contrast Wesley (and Wesleyanism) and Calvin (and Calvinism). Thus, I suggest use of the acrostic ACURA in order to aid people in contrasting Wesleyan beliefs with those of Calvinism and TULIP. Let me juxtapose ACURA and TULIP in the following chart.

Calvinism and Wesleyanism	
Calvinism—TULIP	**Wesleyanism—ACURA**
1. Total depravity	1. All are sinful
2. Unconditional election	2. Conditional election
3. Limited atonement	3. Unlimited atonement
4. Irresistible grace	4. Resistible grace
5. Perseverance of the saints	5. Assurance of salvation

There are a number of other ways that I could have created an acrostic to represent the greater Arminian and Wesleyan traditions. For example, I could use the five terms in the English translation of the Remonstrance, mentioned above. But practically speaking, the letters CUSRT or CUSRU do not easily lend themselves to a memorable acrostic, nor does a reordering of the letters in SCURT or SCURU. The acrostic ACURA may seem a bit cliché, but it is my hope that the simplicity and memorability of the acrostic will aid people in becoming more aware and discursive of its key theological issues related to divine sovereignty, human freedom, and salvation.

For a long time, I have taught about the Synod of Dort and the alternative views of Calvinism and Arminianism. Since the five points of Calvinism are the most widely known, it made more common sense to list the five points of Arminianism (and Wesleyanism) in contrast with the Calvinist views. In fact, for years, a chart I created for teaching about these theological issues used the last four acrostic categories of CURA. With regard to total depravity, Wesley shared probably his greatest agreement with Calvin. Thus, it was a simple matter for me to discuss the first point of contrast with the phrase *all are sinful*. All have sinned, to be sure (Romans 3:23), but Wesley—like Calvin—believed that sin went much deeper. People are thoroughly sinful and incapable of saving themselves, and thus must rely on divine grace for eternal life.

So ACURA represents a catchy acrostic (heuristic tool, or useful myth) for talking about Wesley's view of divine predestination and human freedom with regard to salvation. To the scholar, ACURA may seem too kitschy and lacking in theological precision. To the car enthusiast, the name may also be misleading, though cars produced by the Acura Corporation suggest "accuracy."[6] Be that as it may, because the term *ACURA* is more easily remembered, it has a chance of rivaling TULIP as a mnemonic device for talking about the extremely important—indeed, eternally important—topics of divine predestination, human freedom, and salvation.

More ACURA Than TULIP

Not only do I think that ACURA represents a helpful acrostic for contrasting Wesley's views with those of Calvin and Calvinists; I also believe that its message is more persuasive, more biblical, and truer to life. Throughout this book I have shown my appreciation for Calvin; he contributed tremendously to the theology and historic development of Protestantism. But Calvin does not represent every Christian, especially every Protestant Christian. Moreover, many who call themselves a follower of Calvin or Calvinism may not even live like they say they believe. Too often there occurs a disconnection between what Christians say they believe and value, and how they actually live. For some, this has to do with being hypocritical. But for others, and I suspect the larger number, they have accepted Calvinistic and Reformed theology without really thinking about how relevant such theology is to the ways they believe as well as live their lives in practice. They just may have not had the time (or taken the time and effort) to think self-critically and consider unmistakable biblical alternatives, or had the courage to modify their *theory* to match their *practice*.

I am so convinced that Wesley did a better job of capturing the heart of the Bible and of articulating how the Holy Spirit continues to work daily in the lives of people that I cannot help recommend "more ACURA and less TULIP." If you believe in (1) total depravity, (2) unconditional election, (3) limited atonement, (4) irresistible grace, and (5) perseverance of the saints, then you will most likely affirm TULIP. But I suspect that many do not affirm the aforementioned doctrines. Moreover, if Christians affirm one, two, or only a part of a third point of Calvinism, then they need to reconsider the relevance of their basic beliefs and values. After all, the theory you hold (your beliefs and values) powerfully affects how you live day by day, whether it occurs consciously or unconsciously. If you believe more in the doctrines that (1) all are sinful, (2) conditional election, (3) unlimited atonement, (4) resistible grace, and (5) assurance of salvation, then you should definitely affirm ACURA.

Wesley had an uncanny ability to discern the heart of biblical teachings and make them practically relevant to people in general and to Christians in particular. He was methodical in his theology and ministry, though not in the sense of being a Christian system-maker, especially when system making trumped the reality of biblical teachings and the complexities of life. Life can be quite messy, after all—quite unsystematic and unpredictable. We need to be attentive to the Holy Spirit and be ready to respond deftly to the spiritual, physical, social, and other needs that people experience. Yet, because we are not alone but have the ever-present grace of God in our lives, we may boldly live in ways that are free and in which we may responsibly choose to partake of the many divine blessings promised to us. Such blessings include salvation as well as holy living that reflect love for God and our neighbors, socially as well as individually. May we as Christians always endeavor, by the grace of God, to bring our beliefs more in line with our practice.

Discussion Questions

1. Do you understand the five points of Calvinism—TULIP? With which of the five points do you agree the most? With which do you disagree?

2. Do you understand the five points of Arminianism? With which of the five points do you agree the most? With which do you disagree?

3. With which theology do you agree the most: Arminianism or Calvinism? Why?

4. How has misunderstanding of the five points been damaging to Arminianism? Has it also been damaging to Calvinism?

5. Is the acrostic ACURA helpful in comparing Wesley and Calvin? What are its benefits, and what are its liabilities?

6. Does the discussion of the five points help you to bring your beliefs more in line with your practice?

NOTES

Preface

1. E. Glenn Hinson, "A Contemplative Response," in *Christian Spirituality: Five Views of Sanctification,* ed. Donald L. Alexander (Downers Grove, IL: Inter Varsity Press, 1988), 129.

Introduction: Christians Live More Like Wesley Than Calvin

1. John Wesley, *Works* 21, *Journal* 14th May 1765, Letter to John Newton. (Note: A period that does not appear in the original letter has been added after the word *Mr.*) Although Wesley agreed with much of what Calvin believed, Wesley also disagreed with much of it.

2. Be aware that more Catholic traditions exist than only the Roman Catholic Church. But in most cases I use the word *Catholic* to refer to the beliefs, values, and practices of the Roman Catholic Church.

3. John Wesley, "Thoughts on Salvation by Faith," §5, *Works* (Jackson), XI:493–94.

4. Wesley, "Preface," §6, *Sermons, Works,* 1.103–4.

5. William J. Abraham, *The Coming Great Revival: Recovering the Full Evangelical Tradition* (San Francisco: Harper & Row, 1984), 67.

6. Wesley, "Preface," §2, in *Sermons, Works* (1.103–4).

7. Some scholars describe Wesley's references to a right heart (*orthokardia*) as right affections or tempers (*orthoaffectus*) or right passions (*orthopathia*).

8. I first suggested this acrostic in a book I wrote with Steve Wilkens entitled *Everything You Know about Evangelicals Is Wrong (Well, Almost Everything): An Insider's Look at Myths and Realities* (Grand Rapids: Baker Academic, 2010), 212, n. 12.

Chapter 1. God: More Love Than Sovereignty

1. Calvin, *Institutes*, I.i.1 (1.35).

2. Ibid., I.xvi.3 (1.200).

3. Ibid., I.xvi.4 (1.201–2).

4. Ibid., I.xviii.2 (1.232).

5. Ibid., III.xxi.7 (2.931).

6. Ibid., III.xxviii.1 (2.947).

7. Ibid., III.xxviii.7 (2.955). The Latin phrase *decretum horribile*, which Calvin used, is sometimes translated as "horrible decree" or "awe-inspiring." Calvin used it to describe the doctrine of reprobation, but others have used the phrase to describe his entire theology of divine predestination, election, and reprobation.

8. Ibid., I.xiv.16 (1.175).

9. Ibid., I.v.1 (1.52).

10. Ibid., III.xxi.1 (2.922–23).

11. Wesley, "Thoughts upon God's Sovereignty," *Works* (Jackson), 10.361.

12. Wesley, "The Unity of the Divine Being," §5, *Works* (Jackson), VII.265.

13. Ibid., §7, 7.266.

14. Wesley, "Predestination Calmly Considered," §45, *Works* (Jackson), (10.229–30).

15. Wesley, "Thoughts upon God's Sovereignty," *Works* (Jackson), 10.362.

16. Wesley, *NT Notes*, 1 John 4:8.

17. Calvin, *Institutes*, I.v.3 (1.55).

18. Ibid., II.xvi.4 (1.506).

19. Wesley, "New Creation," §18, *Works*, 2:510.

20. Wesley, "Some Remarks on 'A Defence of the Preface to the Edinburgh Edition of Aspasio Vindicated'," §6, *Works* (Jackson), 10:351. Words in brackets are mine.

21. Wesley, "God's Love to Fallen Man," §5 sermon 59, *Works* (Jackson), (6.235).

22. Wesley, "Predestination Calmly Considered," §42 *Works* (Jackson), 10.227.

23. Ibid.

24. Wesley, "Free Grace," §§23, 25 *Works* (Jackson), 7.381, 383.

25. Charles Wesley, "Free Grace" (hymn XVI), in *Hymns on God's Everlasting Love* (Bristol: Felix Farley and Sons, 1741); reprinted in *The Poetical Works of John and Charles Wesley*, vol. 3, ed. G. Osborn (London: Wesleyan-Methodist Conference Office, 1869), 96.

26. Philip Schaff, *History of the Christian Church*, 8 vols. (1910 reprint; Grand Rapids: Eerdmans, 1976), 8.261.2

Chapter 2. Bible: More Primary Than Sole Authority

1. Calvin, *Institutes,* I.vi.1 (1.70).

2. Ibid., I.vii.5 (1.80).

3. Ibid., I.viii.4 (1.78).

4. Ibid., I.viii.5 (1.85–86) and I.ix.1 (1.93).

5. Raymond A. Blacketer, "Commentaries and Prefaces," in *The Calvin*

Handbook, ed. Herman J. Selderhuis (Grand Rapids: Eerdmans, 2009), 184.

6. Calvin, *Institutes,* I.ix.1 (1.94).

7. Martin Luther, quoted by Erwin Iserloh, Joseph Glazik, and Hubert Jedin, *Reformation and Counter Reformation,* trans. Anselm Biggs and Peter W. Becker, in *History of the Church,* vol. V, ed. Hubert Jedin and John Dolan (English translation 1980; reprint, New York: Crossroad, 1986), 79.

8. Ibid., n. 17.

9. Calvin, *Institutes,* I.vi.2 (1.72).

10. Ibid., IV.viii.8 (2.1155).

11. Wesley, "Preface," §5, *Sermons, Works,* 1.105.

12. Wesley, "The Character of a Methodist," §1, in *Works* (Jackson), 8:340.

13. Wesley, "To Thomas Whitehead," 10 February 1748, *Letters* (Telford), 2.117.

14. Wesley, "A Clear and Concise Demonstration of the Divine Inspiration of the Holy Scriptures," *Works* (Jackson), 11.484.

15. Wesley, "Minutes of Several Conversations," Q.32, *Works* (Jackson), 8.315.

16. Henry R. McAdoo, *The Spirit of Anglicanism: A Survey of Anglican Theological Method in the Seventeenth Century* (New York: Scribner's, 1965), 313.

17. Wesley, "Preface," §6, *Works* (Jackson), 1.iv.

18. Wesley, "On Laying the Foundation of the New Chapel" (1777, sermon 112), II.3, *Works,* 3:586.

19. Wesley, "Address to the Clergy," I.2, *Works* (Jackson), 10.483.

20. Wesley, "To Dr. Rutherford," 28 March 1768, *Letters* (Telford), 5.364. Words in brackets are mine.

21. Wesley, "Preface," §6, *Sermons, Works,* 1.106.

22. Wesley, "A Farther Appeal to Men of Reason and Religion, Part I," V.24, *Works,* 11.167. Words in brackets are mine.

23. Albert C. Outler, "The Wesleyan Quadrilateral in John Wesley," *Wesleyan Theological Journal* 20, no. 1 (Spring 1985): 11.

24. For more information about the Wesleyan quadrilateral, see Don Thorsen, *The Wesleyan Quadrilateral* (Grand Rapids: Zondervan, 1990), and W. Stephen Gunter et al., *Wesley and the Quadrilateral* (Nashville: Abingdon Press, 1997).

25. Thorsen, *Wesleyan Quadrilateral,* 248.

Chapter 3. Humanity: More Freedom Than Predestination

1. Calvin, *Institutes,* I.xv.3 (1.186).

2. Wesley, "The New Birth," I.1, *Works,* 2.188.

3. Calvin, *Institutes,* II.i.8 (1.251).

4. Wesley, "The Image of God," ii.2-5, *Works,* 4.298–99.

5. Calvin, *Institutes,* III.xxii.8 (2.957).

6. Ibid., I.xv.8 (1.196).

7. Ibid., I.xviii.2 (1.232).

8. Ibid., I.xvi.8 (1.207).

9. Ibid., III.xxi.5 (2.926).

10. Methodist Episcopal Church, *The Articles of Religion,* 1784/1804, article 7: "Of Original or Birth Sin," in *Creeds and Confessions of Faith in the Christian Tradition,* vol. III, part 5, *Statements of Faith in Modern Christianity,* ed. Jaroslav Pelikan and Valerie Hotchkiss (New Haven: Yale University Press, 2003), 203.

11. Wesley, "A Dialogue between a Predestinarian and His Friend," *Works* (Jackson), 10.265.

12. Wesley, "Thoughts Upon Necessity," iii.7, *Works* (Jackson), 10.467. Words in brackets are mine.

13. Calvin, *Institutes,* III.xxiv.17 (2.985).

14. Ibid., III.xxiv.12 (2.978).

15. Wesley, "Free Grace," §9, sermon 110, *Works* 3.547. I add the words "preterition or single predestination," which Wesley mentioned in the following paragraph.

16. Ibid., §9, 3.547.

17. Wesley, "Predestination Calmly Considered,"§58, *Works* (Jackson), 10.238.

18. Ibid., §18, *Works* (Jackson), 10.210.

19. Ibid., §37, *Works* (Jackson), 10.224.

20. Wesley, "The Consequence Proved," §8, *Works* (Jackson), 10:373–74. Words in brackets are mine.

21. Wesley, "Free Grace," §§1–3, *Works,* 3.544–55.

22. Ibid., §3, *Works,* 3.545.

23. Wesley, "Predestination Calmly Considered," §49, *Works* (Jackson), 10.231.

24. Calvin, *Institutes,* I.xvi.9 (1.210).

25. Wesley, "A Plain Account of Christian Perfection," *Works* (Jackson), 11.430.

Chapter 4. Grace: More Prevenient Than Irresistible

1. Calvin, *Institutes,* III.xiii.5 (1.768).

2. Ibid., II.iii.13 (1.308).

3. Ibid., I.ii.6 (1.263).

4. Ibid., II.v.13 (1.333). Words in brackets are mine.

5. Wesley, "Working Out Our Own Salvation," II.1, sermon 85, *Works* (Jackson), 6.509.

6. Ibid., III.7, *Works* (Jackson), 6.513.

7. Calvin, *Institutes,* I.xvi.9 (1.208–9).

8. Wesley, "Predestination Calmly Considered," §41, *Works* (Jackson), 10.226–27.

9. Ibid., §42, *Works* (Jackson), 10.227.

10. Calvin, *Institutes,* II.ii.17 (1.276).

11. Ibid., II.ii.17 (1.276).

12. Ibid., II.ii.17 (1.276–77). Cf. *Institutes* IV.xx.15–16 (2.1503–05).

13. Wesley, "Working Out Our Own Salvation," II.1, sermon 85, *Works* (Jackson), 6.509.

14. Calvin, *Institutes,* IV.iv.1 (2.1012). Words in brackets are mine. In footnote 2, the editor, John McNeill, provides the full quotation from Cyprian: "You cannot have God for your Father unless you have the church for your Mother."

15. Ibid., IV.iv.5 (2.1017).

16. Ibid., IV.xiv.6 (2.1281).

17. Ibid.

18. Calvin offers several arguments in defense of infant baptism. See Ibid., IV.16.1–32 (2.1303–23).

19. Wesley, "The Means of Grace," II.1, sermon 16, *Works,* 1.381.

20. Wesley, "Minutes of Several Conversations," Q.48, *Works* (Jackson), 8.322–23.

21. Ibid., 8.323–24.

Chapter 5. Salvation: More Unlimited Than Limited

1. Wesley, *Journal* (Curnock ed.), 1:475–76.

2. Calvin, "Preface," *Commentary on the Book of Psalms,* vol. 1, trans. James Anderson (Grand Rapids: Eerdmans, 1948), xl–xli.

3. Calvin, quoted by Bruce Gordon, *Calvin* (New Haven: Yale University Press, 2009), 34.

4. Calvin, *Institutes,* II.xvii.5 (1.509–10).

5. Wesley, "The Doctrine of Original Sin," pt. V, *Works* (Jackson), 9:412.

6. Wesley, *NT Notes,* 1 John 2:2.

7. Calvin, *Institutes,* III.xxi.7 (2.931).

8. Calvin, *Commentaries,* John 3:16. Cf. Calvin's comments upon 1 John 2:1-2, which suggests unlimited atonement.

9. Ibid.

10. Wesley, "Free Grace," §30, *Works,* 3.559–63.

11. For more information about the doctrine of limited atonement, see the appendix.

12. Calvin, *Institutes,* III.xi.10 (1.737).

13. Ibid., III.xi.2 (1.727).

14. Ibid., III.xi.3 (1.728).

15. Ibid., III.xviii.8 (1.830).

16. Ibid., III.xi.6 (1.723).

17. Ibid., II.v.3 (1.320).

18. Ibid., III.ii.11 (1.556). Words in brackets are mine.

19. Wesley, "Salvation by Faith," §3, sermon 1, *Works,* 1.118.

20. Wesley, "Thoughts on Salvation by Faith," §10, *Works* (Jackson), 11.495.

21. Wesley, "The Scripture Way of Salvation," I.3, sermon 43, *Works,* 2.157.

22. Calvin, *Institutes,* III.ii.16 (1.562).

23. Ibid., III.xiv.20 (1.787).

24. See The Westminster Confession of Faith, 1647, chap. 18, "Of the Assurance of Grace and Salvation," in *Creeds and Confessions of Faith in the Christian Tradition,* vol. II, part 4, *Creeds and Confessions of the Reformation Era,* ed. Jaroslav Pelikan and Valerie Hotchkiss (New Haven: Yale University Press, 2003), 627–28.

25. Wesley, "The Witness of the Spirit, II," II.2, sermon 11, *Works,* 1.287.

26. See Wesley, "On Faith," I.10–13, *Works* (Jackson), 7.198–200.

27. Wesley, "The Witness of the Spirit, II," I.4, sermon 11, *Works,* 1.285.

Chapter 6. Spirituality: More Holiness Than Mortification

1. Calvin, *Institutes,* II.viii.51 (1.415).

2. Ibid., III.iii.3 (1.595).

3. Ibid., III.xx.46 (2.913).

4. Ibid., III.xx.2, 10 (2.851, 862).

5. Ibid., III.xx.27 (2.886).

6. Ibid., III.xx.3 (2.852).

7. Ibid., II.vii.29 (1.396).

8. Ibid., III.iii.11 (1.603).

9. Ibid., II.viii.1 (1.713).

10. Ibid., II.vii.52 (1.416).

11. Ibid., III.xviii.1 (1.822).

12. Ibid., III.xx.52 (2.919).

13. Ibid., III.xx.46 (2.913).

14. Ibid., IV.xv.12 (2.1313).

15. Ibid., III.iii.10 (1.602).

16. Ibid., III.iii.14 (1.606).

17. Ibid., III.iii.20 (1.615).

18. Ibid., III.ii.12 (1.557).

19. Ibid., IV.xv.5 (2.1307).

20. Ibid., IV.xvi.20 (2.1343).

21. Wesley "Preface," §1, *Hymns and Sacred Poems, Works* (Jackson), 14.328.

22. Wesley, *A Plain Account of Christian Perfection: As Believed and Taught*

by the Reverend Mr. John Wesley from the Year 1725 to the Year 1777 (Kansas City: Beacon Hill Press of Kansas City, 1966), 11.

23. Wesley, "On Faith," I.10–13, *Works* (Jackson), 7.198–200.

24. Wesley, *A Plain Account of Christian Perfection: As Believed and Taught by the Reverend Mr. John Wesley from the Year 1725 to the Year 1777* (Kansas City: Beacon Hill Press of Kansas City, 1966), 12. Words in brackets are mine.

25. Wesley, "A Plain Account of Christian Perfection," §13, *Works* (Jackson), 11.379–80.

Chapter 7. Church: More Catholic Than Magisterial

1. Calvin, *Institutes,* IV (2.1011).

2. Ibid., IV.i.9 (2.1023).

3. Ibid., IV.i.4 (2.1016).

4. Ibid., "John Calvin to the Reader" (1.4).

5. Ibid., IV.i.5 (2.1017).

6. Ibid., IV.i.5 (2.1018).

7. Ibid., IV.iii.11 (1052).

8. Ibid., IV.vii.20 (2.1139).

9. Ibid., IV.ii–xi (2.1041–229).

10. For example, see the editorial comments by Beveridge and Bonnet about the letter Calvin wrote to William Farel regarding the joint ecclesial and civil execution of Michael Servetus. See letter, "To Farel," CCCXXXI, *Works,* 5.436, n. 2: "The error of Calvin in the death of Servetus was, we may say, altogether that of his age, inasmuch as men of the most conciliating and moderate dispositions, viz., Bucer, Œcolampadius, Melanchthon, and Bullinger, were at one in their approval of the condemnation of the unfortunate Spanish innovator. One may deeply deplore this error without insulting the Reformation, and combine in a just measure that pity which a great victim demands, with respect for those men whom an unhappy time made the accusers and the judges of Servetus."

11. See Calvin, "The Discipline of the Church: Its Chief Use in Censures and Excommunication," *Institutes,* IV.xii (2.1229–54).

12. See Calvin's letters to Simon Sulzer and Heinrich Bullinger arguing for the punishment of Michael Servetus, which contributed to the execution of Servetus. See Calvin, letter "To Sulzer," CCCXXVII, *Works,* 5:427–30; and letter "To Bullinger," CCCXXXVI, *Works,* 5.447.

13. Calvin, *Institutes,* IV.iv, vii, x (2.1489–90, 1492–93, 1497–99).

14. Ibid., IV.xii.1 (2.1229–30).

15. For example, see chapter XII, "Geneva under Calvin's Sway," in John T. McNeill, *The History and Character of Calvinism* (New York: Oxford University Press, 1954), 178–200.

16. For example, see Alister E. McGrath, *A Life of John Calvin: A Study in the Shaping of Western Culture* (Malden, MA: Blackwell, 1990), 116.

17. Calvin, letters "To Farel," CCCXXII, *Works,* 5.417, and "To Farel," CCCXXXI, *Works,* 5.436.

18. Calvin, letter "To Monseigneur, Monseigneur du Poet, Grand Chamberlain of Navarre and Governor of the Town of Montelimart, at Crest," XVII, *Works,* 7.440.

19. Martin Luther, quoted by Juergan L. Neve, *A History of Christian Thought,* vol. 1 (Philadelphia: The Muhlenberg Press, 1946), 285.

20. The Westminster Confession of Faith, 1647, chap. 23, "Of the Civil Magistrate," in *Creeds and Confessions of Faith in the Christian Tradition,* vol. II, part 4, *Creeds and Confessions of the Reformation Era,* ed. Jaroslav Pelikan and Valerie Hotchkiss (New Haven: Yale University Press, 2003), 636.

21. Wesley, "Of the Church," §16, sermon 74, *Works,* 3.51.

22. Wesley, "The Way to the Kingdom," I.6, *Works,* 1.220–21.

23. Wesley, "Of the Church," §16, *Works,* 3.52.

24. Wesley, "A Letter to a Roman Catholic," §16, *Works* (Jackson), 10.85.

25. Wesley, "Catholic Spirit," III.1–3, *Works,* 2.92–93.

26. Ibid, III.4–5, *Works,* 2.94.

27. Wesley, "Causes of the Inefficacy of Christianity," §7, *Works,* 4.90.

28. Wesley, "Dialogue between a Predestinarian and His Friend," *Works* (Jackson), 10.266.

Chapter 8. Ministry: More Empowering Than Triumphal

1. Calvin, *Institutes,* IV.xiv.11 (2.1286). Usually Calvin speaks of "Word and sacraments," referring to the latter term in the plural. With regard to the second of two sacraments, Calvin usually speaks of the "Sacred Supper," but he also refers to it as the "Lord's Supper."

2. John T. McNeill, *The History and Character of Calvinism* (New York: Oxford University Press, 1967), 136.

3. Calvin, *Institutes,* IV.xvi.1–32 (2.1324–59).

4. Ibid., IV.xvii.2 (2.1361).

5. Ibid., IV.i.1 (2.1011–12).

6. Ibid., IV.i.5 (2.1017).

7. Ibid., IV.iii.4 (2.1057).

8. Ibid.

9. John T. McNeill, *Institutes* 2.1057, n. 4. McNeil says: "Referring chiefly to Luther, whom he elsewhere often praises. Cf. Calvin's *Defensio adversus Pighium,* where Luther is called 'a distinguished apostle of Christ by whose ministry the light of the gospel has shone' (CR VI. 250)."

10. Calvin, *Institutes,* IV.iii.5 (2.1058).

11. Ibid., IV.xix.19 (2.1467).

12. Ibid., IV.iii.11 (2.1063).

13. Ibid., IV.xv.21 (2:1321–22).

14. Ibid., IV.iii.4 (2.1057).

15. Wesley, letter to "Dear Sir" (unknown), quoted by Wesley in his *Journal,* 11 June 1739, *Works,* 19.67.

16. Wesley, "Preface," *Hymns and Sacred Poems, Works* (Jackson), 14.321. Wesley's full quotation said: "The gospel of Christ knows of no religion, but social; no holiness but social holiness."

17. References to spiritual gifts are found in Romans 12:6-8; 1 Corinthians 12:4-11, 28; and Ephesians 4:11; references to fruit of the Spirit are found in Galatians 5:22-23.

18. In "an introductory comment" to Wesley's sermon "The Use of Money," Outler said: "These masses were Wesley's self-chosen constituency: 'Christ's poor'"; see *Works,* 2.263.

19. Wesley, "Thoughts upon Slavery," V.6, *Works* (Jackson), 11.79.

20. Wesley, letter "To William Wilberforce," 24 February 1791, *Letters* (Telford) 8.264–65.

Appendix

1. The Canons of the Synod of Dort, 1618-19, in *Creeds and Confessions of Faith in the Christian Tradition,* vol. II, part 4, *Creeds and Confessions of the Reformation Era,* ed. Jaroslav Pelikan and Valerie Hotchkiss (New Haven: Yale University Press, 2003), 571, 572. Hereafter references to The Canons of the Synod of Dort will be referred to as "Canons of Dort."

2. Canons of Dort, II.4.580.

3. Ibid., II.4.583–84.

4. Ibid., II.4.591, 592.

5. The Remonstrance, 1610, in *Creeds and Confessions of Faith in the Christian Tradition,* vol. II, part 4, *Creeds and Confessions of the Reformation Era,* ed. Jaroslav Pelikan and Valerie Hotchkiss (New Haven: Yale University Press, 2003), 549–50.

6. It is my understanding that the Acura Corporation was created in North America in order to sell high-end cars on behalf of the Honda Corporation. The name Acura communicated "accuracy," which reflected the carmaker's motto: "Precision Crafted Performance." Humorously speaking, would you rather have an ACURA or a TULIP?

INDEX

CPSIA information can be obtained
at www.ICGtesting.com
Printed in the USA
LVHW050201070619
620438LV00003B/10/P

9 781426 743351